REAL SIMPLE

solutions

FROM THE EDITORS OF *REAL SIMPLE*

WRITTEN BY AMANDA HINNANT

Some days, life just feels like a series of problems. From dawn (following a bad night's sleep) to dusk (out of milk, again), the small hurdles we all face can make us want to crawl into bed and pull the covers over our heads. (And if you've never had a day like that, check your pulse and e-mail me immediately.)

Needless to say, like people and their expectations, problems come in all different sizes. There are the big, serious, existential problems that—chances are—no book can solve for you. And then there are the nagging, mundane problems that *really* get under your skin: a run in your new stockings, a wax spill on the linen tablecloth, a perpetually missing remote (or four).

Real Simple Solutions will not broker world peace, tell you how to eliminate the common cold from your life, or even begin to address the mystery of why some people never get their wisdom teeth. But for the constant, headache-inducing everyday problems, this book has the answers.

Month after month, *Real Simple* magazine helps its millions of readers navigate life's daily challenges, giving them shortcuts and strategies to get through those long to-do lists and start enjoying their want-to-do lists. *Real Simple Solutions* does the same, only on a larger scale. The book is organized by activity and follows the sequence of an average day (with a special occasion to top it all off). From working to celebrating and everything in between, it presents inspired ideas to make your life easier, calmer, more organized, and more beautiful. You'll find inventive new ways to use household items, quick tips for refreshing your surroundings, foolproof instructions for doing routine tasks, and essential reference information. You may not find the meaning of life in a pile of clean laundry, but let me tell you: When that load of laundry is done, you've got a lot more mental space to start thinking about the Big Issues.

If you have an inexhaustible appetite for easy solutions (and who doesn't?), visit www.realsimple.com, which has a database of literally thousands of searchable ideas, continually updated. And enjoy the surprises on every page of this book. They are guaranteed to improve the quality of your daily life, whether you've had a good night's sleep or not.

Kristin van Ogtrop

MANAGING EDITOR, *REAL SIMPLE*

contents

in every chapter

the organized life
Basic jobs like cooking meals and wrapping gifts can be a piece of cake if you're armed with the right tools and knowledge. This section tells you what essentials to have on hand—and how best to use them.

easy upgrades
From inexpensive additions to your wardrobe to split-second ways to refurbish your rooms, here are scores of inspiring ideas for making the ordinary more extraordinary (without a lot of effort).

crib sheet
Need to know how to remove a ketchup stain? Or what to stock for a party? These reference pages provide all kinds of vital information. Even better: the convenient tear-out versions found at the back of the book.

new uses for old things
Here's where you'll learn how to make objects you already have do something completely different...say, using ice-cube trays to store jewelry, or a can to cut biscuits (as shown, right).

simple technique
Rely on this section's clear, step-by-step instructions to help you master common—but often tricky—tasks, like painting a room or hand washing delicate clothing.

the multitasker
Some everyday items have a *slew* of hidden talents. Each chapter concludes with one of these household aces—a lemon, vinegar, baking soda, even dental floss—and its myriad versatile uses.

grooming

Sometimes tried-and-true routines deserve re-examining. Take your daily beauty rituals, for instance. Just because you've been applying makeup the same way since high school doesn't mean there isn't an easier—and, yes, faster— approach. To that end, the tips on these pages will help you get fabulous in a flash. How's *that* for a makeover?

beauty basics

MAKEUP..

These fundamental products are all you
need for everyday use. When it comes
to picking colors, choose shades very close
to your skin tone to keep your look natural.
Clockwise from top right:

■ **CONCEALER:** It covers redness and
erases dark circles and spots in seconds.

■ **MASCARA:** After curling lashes, brush on
one or two coats to add length and fullness.

■ **LIP COLOR:** Generally, a lipstick will give
you the most saturated color, a gloss
will deliver a shiny (albeit shorter-lasting)
glaze, and a stain will be most enduring.

■ **LIP BALM:** This protects lips from
chapping and cracking and smooths
them out for even lipstick application.

■ **BLUSH:** Sweep it onto the apples of your
cheeks for a healthy flush.

■ **BLOTTING PAPERS:** They deftly diminish
shine without removing makeup.

POWDER BRUSH..

A full-size natural-bristle brush is indispensable for applying blush and powder
evenly and well. It can last a lifetime if
maintained with regular washing: Run
the tips of the bristles under warm water
and massage in a drop of shampoo or
liquid soap. Rinse and air-dry.

TWEEZERS ....

Not only do they neaten brows and pluck
stray hairs, but tweezers also moonlight
as splinter removers. If your pair becomes
dirty and loses its gripping power, wipe
the tips with a cotton ball dipped in
isopropyl alcohol.

EYELASH CURLER ....

Other than your morning cup of coffee (or
another hour of sleep), nothing can help
you look more awake. Use it before applying mascara so you don't soil the pads.

MAKEUP REMOVER

Mild enough to use on the delicate eye area, it also works where soap doesn't— like on waterproof mascara or lip stains. Your pillowcase will thank you.

MOISTURIZER

Any formula will combat flakiness. But dermatologists recommend using one with an SPF of at least 15 to protect against the bigger problem: cancer- and wrinkle-causing UV rays.

BRUSH

For effective yet gentle detangling, pick one with boar bristles (or a nylon-boar combination) set into a rubber cushion. Bonus: Several brushstrokes a day will help keep hair shiny.

FINISHING SPRAY

It adds volume, controls flyaways, and makes styling last longer. Depending on your needs, choose one that leaves hair flexible (for day-to-day use) or one with a stronger hold (for an updo).

CLEAR NAIL POLISH

Nails look neat and natural with a single coat of clear polish. And if you use a quick-dry formula, you'll be good to go in seconds.

NAIL CLIPPERS

Opt for small stainless-steel models, which are easier to maneuver (especially around tiny pinkie toes) and won't rust.

NAIL FILE

To smooth sharp edges and shape, use a large file with a coarse grain on one side and a finer grain on the other.

for your face and hair

DOUBLE IMPACT

To get a warm, rosy glow with depth and staying power, rub cream blush onto the apples of your cheeks with your fingertips, then top with a fine dusting of powder blush in a similar shade.

A BETTER BRONZE

When applying tinted moisturizer, don't forget your earlobes. A hint of color there makes the flush of your face look more natural (and keeps your lobes soft and smooth, to boot).

ONE-MINUTE HAIR REVIVAL

No time to shower? Stretch your hairstyle one more day by sprinkling baby powder on a brush and running it through your hair. (To avoid the powdered-wig look, those with dark hair should use a dry shampoo—sold at drugstores—instead.)

A TWIST ON THE CHIGNON ▶

Say hello to your new go-to updo: Gather hair into a ponytail and pull it halfway through the elastic on the last pass. Then grab the end section of hair, wrap it around the elastic once, and tuck the ends into the elastic (under the knot).

for your body

THE BIG CHILL

During hot summer months, pop your skin-care products—face and body lotions, eye creams, cleansers, toners—in the refrigerator before hopping into the shower. They'll feel even more refreshing after you step out.

SINGLE-SERVING SUNBURN RELIEF

Freeze aloe vera gel (sold at drugstores and health-food stores) in an ice-cube tray for the next time you linger too long at the beach. Skimming an aloe cube over sunburned skin can ease pain, add moisture, and provide that much needed cooling relief.

SOFTEN WHILE YOU WORK

Turn a daily chore into a dry-hand cure. When it's time to wash dishes, apply a generous coat of heavyweight cream to your hands before slipping on your rubber gloves. The heat from the water will help the moisturizer penetrate.

◄ SUPER SKIN SMOOTHER

Before you step into the bathtub, rub in a salt-based body scrub from head to toe. Once you take the plunge, the salt will exfoliate rough patches and then dissolve to soften the bathwater—and further soften your body.

take-care-of-yourself calendar

JANUARY

■ **DON'T FORGET SUNSCREEN.** UV rays are just as potent in winter. To protect yourself, always use a facial moisturizer with an SPF of at least 15.

■ **BUY NEW MASCARA.** If you haven't tossed your mascara since September, do so this month (and again after four more months).

■ **ZAP SKIN SPOTS.** Are spots or broken blood vessels a problem? Consult a dermatologist about laser treatment now. Lasers work best on paler skin because they're drawn to color. If skin is tan, the laser will often attack the skin, not the spot.

FEBRUARY

■ **START ANTI-AGING OR SKIN-CLEARING TREATMENTS LIKE RETIN-A.** They can make skin sun-sensitive, so winter is the best time to use them, because you'll be spending less time outside.

■ **SCHEDULE A FULL-BODY SKIN-CANCER SCAN.** Any time of the year is fine, as long as you have an annual checkup with a dermatologist. If you've had skin cancer in the past, schedule a six-month follow-up in August. Be on the lookout for moles that change color, shape, or size.

MARCH

■ **SPRING-CLEAN YOUR MAKEUP BAG.** Do an inventory and throw out old things. Toss foundations, concealers, and lipsticks that are a year old, mascara that's more than four months old (see January), and anything that looks or smells strange.

■ **TREAT YOURSELF TO A MASSAGE—FROM A FRIEND OR A PRO.** After a long, cold winter, a rubdown will help reinvigorate you—and loosen up your back muscles.

APRIL

■ **TRY AN EASY WARM-WEATHER HAIRSTYLE.** Go for a shorter style, which will take less time to dry. And schedule regular trims every six to eight weeks.

■ **ADJUST YOUR ANTI-AGING REGIMEN.** Consider decreasing the dose of your vitamin A treatment (like Retin-A or Renova) as summer approaches, since these retinoids thin the top layer of skin and make it more prone to sunburn.

MAY

■ **GROOM FEET AND HANDS.** Start shedding tough skin on feet every other day with a foot file or a pumice scrub, because it takes a few weeks to make a noticeable difference. And instead of a splashy coral polish on your fingers and toes, use a pale shade, like sheer beige or pink. It's modern and classic, and won't show cracks or dings.

■ **RETIRE OLD BOTTLES OF SUN-SCREEN.** Its efficacy deteriorates after a few years. Stock up on a new supply of SPF 15 or higher, and apply it liberally. (For a novel use for the old sunscreen, see page 23.)

JUNE

■ **GET A BIKINI WAX.** If you can withstand the unpleasantness, a bikini wax is relatively inexpensive, and the results last much longer than shaving—about four to six weeks.

■ **BRIGHTEN YOUR SMILE.** Summer is an ideal time for one of your biannual dentist checkups, since many patients are on vacation—just make sure your dentist isn't.

■ **REASSESS THE COLOR OF YOUR CONCEALER.** As your skin gets a touch of sun, you may need a slightly darker shade.

For a tear-out version of this crib sheet, see the booklet on the inside back cover.

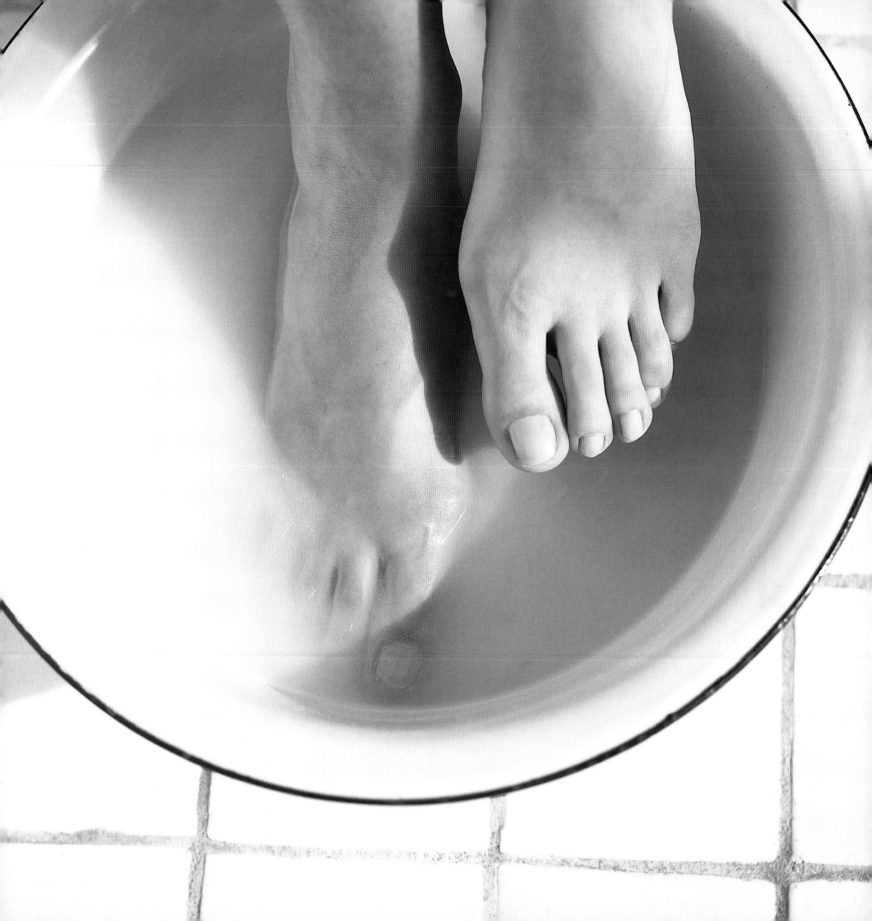

take-care-of-yourself calendar

JULY

■ **PACK A FACE SPRITZER FOR HOT DAYS.** Tote tap water in a spray bottle to keep your skin cool and refreshed (but don't forget to wear waterproof sunscreen).

■ **DEEP-CONDITION HAIR.** Apply an intense hot-oil treatment or mask to wet hair, then wrap in a warm towel. (Toss a damp towel in the microwave for one minute to heat it.) Relax for about 20 minutes, then rinse hair with cool water.

■ **SMOOTH YOUR HEELS.** Bored at the beach? Take a stroll on the sand for natural—and free—exfoliation.

AUGUST

■ **CLEAN YOUR FEET.** After months in flip-flops, your feet may be stained. Fill a basin with equal parts water and hydrogen peroxide, dunk your feet in, and scrub with a nailbrush.

■ **USE A CLARIFYING SHAMPOO FOR A WEEK.** The sun, salt water, and chlorine all take a toll on your hair, leaving it dull, dry, and discolored. A summer-gunk stripper removes all that buildup.

■ **STOCK UP ON MORE SUNSCREEN.** Don't try to make it through Labor Day with an almost empty bottle: You need a shot glass of sunscreen to cover your body with each application.

SEPTEMBER

■ **SWAP IN A RICHER SHADE OF LIPSTICK.** Deep, warm colors work well in cooler weather because they help perk up a pale complexion.

■ **PREVENT NEW-FALL-SHOE BLISTERS.** Walk around in your shoes to identify trouble spots, then put moleskin or a liquid bandage on the areas of your feet liable to blister. (If you do get a small blister, pop it with a sterilized pin, apply ointment, and bandage it.)

OCTOBER

■ **SWITCH TO A NON-WATER-BASED CREAMY CLEANSER.** Bar soap is too drying in cold weather.

■ **SHELVE NAIL POLISH.** Nails need time off to regain their natural color, so leave them clean for a few weeks. Gently buff nail surfaces to remove yellowing.

■ **CLEAR UP SKIN.** You shouldn't expect to clear up blemishes right before the holiday season, since topical antibiotics like benzoyl peroxide take two to three weeks to kick in. To prevent breakouts, start using acne medications now.

NOVEMBER

■ **SPLURGE ON A MANICURE.** Wear nails on the short side to keep them low-maintenance. Take your color of choice with you to the nail appointment (or buy a bottle when you're there), then use it to touch up chips as they occur.

■ **DEEP-CLEAN YOUR PORES.** Schedule a professional facial to brighten skin for the holidays, and do it a couple of days before a party so any irritation from extractions or peels will have disap-peared. After late nights or alcohol consumption, smooth on a nourishing mask.

DECEMBER

■ **DON'T STAIN YOUR TEETH.** Dark bever-ages, such as cranberry juice and red wine, are potential tainters. Rule of thumb: If it's hard to get off your kitchen countertop, it's hard to get off your teeth. After a meal, brush or swish with a mouthwash.

■ **KEEP SKIN MOISTURIZED.** Take quick showers that aren't too steamy, because prolonged exposure to hot water can dry out skin. Exfo-liate with a hydrating scrub, then rub in a rich moisturizer while skin is still damp.

19

lip balm

OLD USE: Skier's sidekick.

NEW USE: Multipurpose beauty lifesaver. Rub it on dry cuticles, elbows, and other rough patches for spot moisturizing. Use it to erase mascara smudges, tame unruly eyebrows, and control flyaways. Lip balm can also help coax a stubborn ring off a swollen finger.

sugar

OLD USE: Medicine chaser.

NEW USE: Lip exfoliator. To smooth dry, peeling lips, try this antidote: Make a paste of sugar and petroleum jelly, then gently massage the concoction into your lips using a toothbrush. Wipe off the excess with a washcloth.

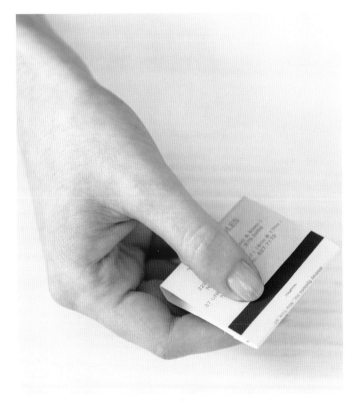

matchbook

OLD USE: Fire lighter.

NEW USE: On-the-go nail file. The matchbook's striker is a smart substitute when you forget a file while traveling and for times when you don't want to whip out the heavy artillery (like at a restaurant).

instant oatmeal

OLD USE: Quick and easy breakfast.

NEW USE: All-natural do-it-yourself facial. Add warm water to a package of unsweetened instant oatmeal, then apply it to your face for 5 to 10 minutes to soothe and hydrate dry skin. But be careful if you leave the bathroom: Oatmeal may dive-bomb the carpet.

tissue paper

OLD USE: Christmas-present cushioning.

NEW USE: Mascara-wand cleaner. When the wand and brush get gunky, rely on a piece of (lint-free) gift-wrapping tissue to wipe away the clumps.

baby oil

OLD USE: 1970s beach-bag staple.

NEW USE: Tar remover. Stick this former tanning agent back in your beach bag, because it's great for getting rid of tar that has glommed on to your bare soles. Smelly turpentine need not apply.

water

OLD USE: Pool filler.

NEW USE: Style booster. If you don't want to pile on more hair products halfway through the day, let water reactivate what you applied in the morning. Just spritz hair and reshape. If you need a firm hold, however, you'll need a fresh coat of hair spray.

last summer's sunscreen

OLD USE: Shelf-space monopolizer.

NEW USE: Shaving lotion. While a bottle of expired sunscreen will no longer protect you from UV rays, it can still protect you from razor burn. Use it when lubing up to keep legs smooth all year long.

how to wash your face

WASH YOUR HANDS

It may seem counterintuitive, but you should do this first—otherwise all that dirt and bacteria will wind up on your face. Use an eye-makeup remover for the area around your eyes, because facial cleansers can be too harsh.

CLEANSE GENTLY

Wet your face with warm—not hot—water. (Hot water strips skin of its protective oils, leaving it fragile and dry.) Lather a nickel-size amount of cleanser between your damp hands, then, using your fingertips, massage it into your skin with a circular motion. Don't rub too aggressively, and don't reach for the washcloth: It can chafe your skin and harbor bacteria between washings.

BE THOROUGH

When applying cleanser, start at your forehead, then move down your nose, across your cheeks, and down to your chin. Don't neglect your hairline, eyebrows, and neck. You should massage your face with cleanser for about 30 seconds to sufficiently loosen dirt and make sure you've covered all areas.

RINSE COMPLETELY

Wash the cleanser off by repeatedly splashing cool water over your face. Plan to spend more time rinsing than cleaning, because cleanser residue can irritate the skin. Next, blot your face and neck with a soft towel. If your skin is oily, dry your face completely before you apply moisturizer. If you have dry skin, dab with a towel until it is almost dry, then seal in dampness with moisturizer.

1 2

3 4

baking soda

SKIN SMOOTHER
For a low-cost, low-tech face scrub, mix three parts baking soda with one part water and massage gently into the skin with a circular motion.

SCRIBBLE ERASER
Sprinkle baking soda on a damp sponge and use it to remove crayon, pencil, and ink marks from painted surfaces. Wipe off the residue.

SCOURING AGENT
Cover stubborn baked-on spots in casserole dishes with baking soda. Let sit for five minutes, then scrub with a damp sponge and rinse.

◄ LINEN FRESHENER
Place an open box of baking soda alongside your stacks of sheets and towels to stave off mustiness.

TOOTH CLEANER
If you're out of toothpaste, mix baking soda with water for an effective, nonabrasive cleanser.

DRAIN UNCLOGGER
Pour one cup of baking soda down the drain, then chase with one cup of vinegar. Let sit for five minutes. Follow with a gallon of boiling water.

STAIN REMOVER
Clean discolored teacups and teapots by making a paste of baking soda and water. Gently rub over the stain to remove.

getting dressed

Your mother, of course, was right: You should take pride in your appearance. There is no pride to be had, however, in early-morning meltdowns, when you're digging through the hamper for that missing sock. Luckily, if you know a few style-wise strategies, you (and your clothes) can look sharp with none of the struggle. Even Mom would be proud.

useful wardrobe savers

KEY PHONE NUMBERS ....

Need to know if your dress—now at the dry cleaner—will be ready for the weekend? Or if the tailor can speed up that alteration? Write the phone numbers of your clothing contacts on a card, and post it on a bulletin board inside your closet door with other wardrobe essentials.

EXTRA BUTTONS, BEADS, AND THREAD ....

These invaluable spares inevitably migrate from the top of your dresser to the back of a drawer to, finally, the trash— unless they have a home. Keep extras for the same garment pinned up together.

WASHING LABELS ....

If a label is itchy, unsightly, or hanging on by a thread, cut it off with scissors or a seam ripper and pin it on the board (if you think you'll forget which piece of clothing it came from, use a permanent marker to identify it). You retain the washing instructions, but your neck doesn't have to endure the irritation.

RECEIPTS ....

Save the ones for recently purchased or expensive items. That way, when those new pants don't fit right or that pricey cashmere sweater starts pilling the first time it's worn, you'll be able to replace the item or get a refund.

LINT ROLLER ....

Hang this fuzz buster over the closet doorknob, and use it to give your outfit the once-over before heading out the door.

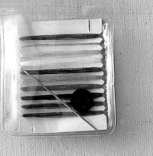

TAILOR - # 313 - 677 - 8093
DRY CLEANER - # 313 - 944 - 48?1
SHOE REPAIR - # 313 - 865 - 1322

RECEIPTS

SUBTOTAL   6.38
8.625% N.Y. TAX   .55
TOTAL   6.93
CHARGE
ACCT   *2003
EXPIRATION DATE: 11/06
Auth Code: 500991
Sequence #6952

CHANGE   .00

WASHING INSTRUCTIONS ON BACK

STITCH WITCHERY

This two-minute miracle worker (sold at craft stores) makes fabric stick to itself to form a permanent bond. It does wonders for fallen hems and pocket flaps that won't stay closed.

HOTEL SEWING KIT

Certain repair jobs make lugging out the Singer seem like overkill. For a loose or missing button, these free sewing kits contain a needle and just the right amount of thread in a rainbow of shades.

MINI SCISSORS

Have a pair of small scissors on hand to safely and effectively remove tags, washing labels, and loose threads.

SAFETY PINS

Elusive when you need them (yet strangely abundant when you don't), safety pins are perfect pinch hitters—they'll keep a wrap top in place, reattach a strap, or stand in for a missing button. Stick a variety of sizes on strips of ribbon.

for clothes

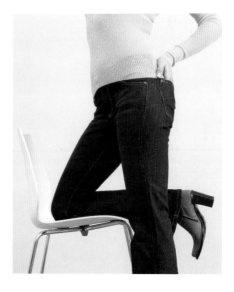

SLIMMER SILHOUETTE

Pants pockets tend to bunch or bow out, adding width where it is least wanted. Have them stitched closed by a tailor (or, if you're handy, do it yourself) to make the shape more streamlined.

OLD COAT, NEW LIFE

Weary of your tired winter wool number? You can revive it—or an old blazer or peacoat—with a quick switch of buttons. Try disks in a contrasting color, vintage-looking rhinestone styles, or elegant iridescent shell versions (shown above).

INSTANT LIVED-IN DENIM

New jeans don't have to be stiff and scratchy. To make just-purchased duds feel like you've owned them forever, remove them from the dryer when still damp and wear them for a couple of hours; the heat of your body will help mold them to your shape.

A TOUCH OF COLOR ▶

For a cheerful addition to any neutral outfit, weave a simple strip of ribbon through your belt loops and tie the ends in a bow. (You'll need about two yards of wide grosgrain.) To prevent fraying, apply a little clear glue to the ribbon's ends.

for accessories

SHOE ADDITIONS

Restrain yourself: Before wearing a new pair of shoes even once, take them to a cobbler and have rubber soles and heel tips attached. The extra layers add traction, protect shoes from the elements, and ensure they will last longer.

ADDED FLAIR

One brooch is nice; three brooches are novel. Cluster a trio of them—here, a velvet flower, a ceramic bird, and a jeweled spider—on a dress, top, skirt, or coat for a one-of-a-kind bouquet.

CLIP ART

Don't know what to do with Grandma's classic clip-on earrings? Clamp the costume-style sparklers onto plain pumps to make the shoes more festive. Position them slightly off-center for a contemporary look—and so they'll peek out from beneath your trousers.

◄ **PURSE REFURBISHMENT**

Sure, it would be nice to buy a new handbag for each season, but what is the point of a new bag if the wallet inside is empty? Instead, refresh your favorite staple by tying a seasonally appropriate scarf around the handle.

foolproof clothing fixes

PROBLEM:

Warped leather bag

SOLUTION:

If the bag is unlined, wipe down its leather insides with a solution of five parts white vinegar to one part water; this will make it more flexible. Then stuff the interior with tissue paper until it's back to its old self. (Let it air out afterward to get rid of any lingering vinegar smell.) If the bag is lined, let it stand, stuffed with tissue paper, for a few days. Or just tote it: Daily carrying can often help a bag return to its natural shape.

PROBLEM:

Snag in a sweater

SOLUTION:

Cutting a snag off can create a hole, so use a sewing needle to push the loose bit through to the inside of the garment, whether it's wool or delicate silk. If the snag is difficult to push through, thread the needle with a similar-colored thread and sew through the snag to grab it. Keep a snag from reappearing by tying it in a knot or dabbing it with clear nail polish—but only if the garment is made of a fabric thick enough that the polish won't bleed through.

PROBLEM:

Lint on clothing

SOLUTION:

The best weapon against fuzz is a lint roller. But in a pinch, you can make do with a mailing label, the sticky back of a FedEx address window envelope, or packing tape wrapped around your hand, with the adhesive side out. For fabrics that aren't washed often, however, use these improvised methods with caution: They may leave behind a residue that will eventually attract more lint.

PROBLEM:

Stubborn zipper

SOLUTION:

If it's sticking, rub the trouble spot with a dry, waxy lubricant, like a candle, lip balm, or soap. But don't get any on the fabric, since it can cause a stain. If the zipper insists on sliding too far down and has to be fished out of a seam, sew across the zipper—teeth and all—at the point you'd like it to stop.

PROBLEM:

Mildew

SOLUTION:

Mildew and its odor are very difficult to remove. Give these tips a try: Soak white washable garments in warm water with a few capfuls of bleach. Colored washables should be machine washed, then soaked overnight in a solution of two ounces of a detergent with color-safe bleach to every gallon of warm water, and machine washed again. Lay white nonwashable garments in the sun (a natural bleacher and deodorizer) for several days. Bring colored nonwashables to the dry cleaner.

PROBLEM:

Ill-fitting sunglasses

SOLUTION:

If your plastic-framed shades have become bent or twisted, skip the emergency trip to the sunglasses shop and perform this at-home adjustment: Immerse the sunglasses in hot water or blast them with a hair dryer until the plastic starts to get flexible, then slowly and gently bend the frame back into shape.

For a tear-out version of this crib sheet, see the booklet on the inside back cover.

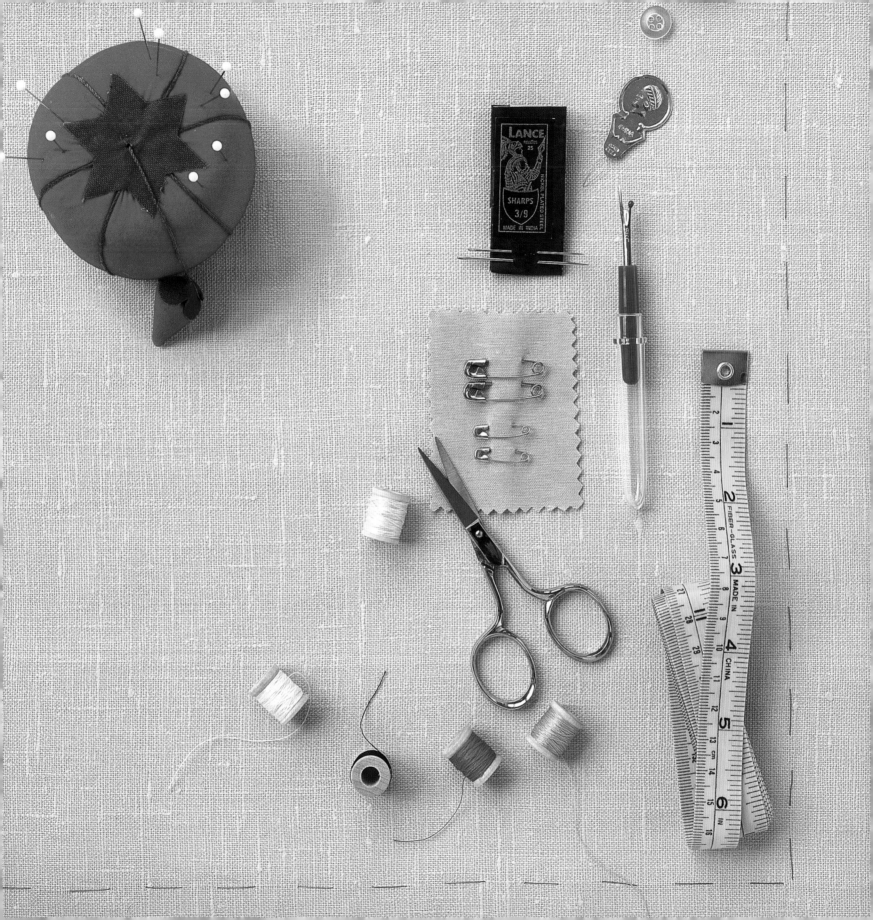

foolproof clothing fixes

PROBLEM:
Hosiery run

SOLUTION:
You guessed it: Brush on some clear nail polish to stop a run in its tracks. Gently pull the nylon away from your leg while you apply the polish, then give it a few seconds to dry before letting go. That way the fabric won't stick to your skin—and do further damage when it's time to take the stockings off.

PROBLEM:
Stretched-out cuffs

SOLUTION:
Once sleeve cuffs start to go slack, there's no surefire way to restore their elasticity. But you can temporarily tighten loose cuffs on a wool or cotton sweater by dampening them with hot water, then drying them with a hair dryer. The hot water and the dryer's heat work together to cause shrinkage. Sometimes just running a hot iron along the cuffs is enough to contract the fabric for a while.

PROBLEM:
Scratched shoes

SOLUTION:
Before treating a nick or a scratch on leather shoes or a bag, it's important to test-treat a hidden spot, like the inside of a handle or strap or underneath a buckle. For the safest form of scratch removal, try dabbing the scratch and the surrounding leather with a little white vinegar to swell the area (think accessory collagen). Let it dry, then buff the item with colorless shoe polish. Feeling bolder? Carefully fill in the scratch using a permanent felt-tip pen in the same color.

PROBLEM:
Perspiration stains

SOLUTION:
These unattractive yellow stains are almost impossible to erase completely (particularly when they're on light-colored clothing), but there are tricks to making them fade. If the fabric is washable, apply a 3 percent hydrogen peroxide solution to the stain, then machine wash the garment in warm water. Bring nonwashables to the dry cleaner.

PROBLEM:
Hanger dimples

SOLUTION:
Clothes hangers, especially wire ones, can leave unwanted puckers at the shoulders of sweaters and other impressionable garments. To work the dimples out, lay the item flat, then give it a blast of steam from a steamer or an iron. Or place it on a towel in the bathroom while you take a hot shower.

PROBLEM:
Dull jewelry

SOLUTION:
The best way to clean and brighten all kinds of jewelry is to scrub them with a soft toothbrush dipped in warm water that's been spiked with a few drops of dishwashing liquid. For plain silver jewelry without gemstones or intricate patterns, a quick-shine strategy is to soak the items in a mixture of $1/2$ cup of warm water, three to four drops of dishwashing liquid, and one drop of ammonia.

pumice stone

OLD USE: Callus reducer.

NEW USE: Pill remover. When your wool sweater has generated a furry outer layer, firmly brush it with the stone and the pills will slough off.

soda bottle

OLD USE: Soft-drink container.

NEW USE: Boot supporter. Insert an empty one-liter plastic bottle into a tall boot to keep it from sagging, creasing, or toppling over. Bonus: Upright boots create space on your closet floor to fill as you please (hmm... more boots?).

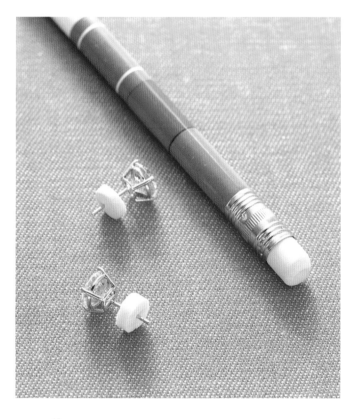

pencil eraser

OLD USE: Mistake corrector.

NEW USE: Earring securer. If the backing for one of your studs goes AWOL, slice off a disk-shaped wedge from an eraser. The earring will stay put—even if your pencil looks denuded.

wire hanger

OLD USE: Dry-cleaning holder.

NEW USE: Static defuser. To tame a skirt that's clinging indelicately to your legs, run the long side of a hanger over the surface and then underneath. It will discharge the garment sans smelly chemical sprays.

lightbulb

OLD USE: Room illuminator.

NEW USE: Ribbon dewrinkler. Slide a ribbon over a recently turned-on lightbulb to smooth it out. Make sure the ribbon isn't made of a synthetic material and the lightbulb isn't too hot (otherwise you risk melting the fabric).

salad spinner

OLD USE: Lettuce tumbler.

NEW USE: Cashmere dryer. Save time—and your sweater's shape—by gently spinning off excess water before laying the garment flat to dry. (Just don't use this trick with loose-knit or especially delicate items, since they can snag or get stretched out.)

ice-cube tray

OLD USE: Water solidifier.

NEW USE: Jewelry organizer. Devote separate cubbies
to your necklaces, bracelets, rings, and pairs of earrings,
and stack multiple trays as needed. Then say so long
to knotted chains and nomadic hoops.

gym sock

OLD USE: Sweat absorber.

NEW USE: Shoe protector. Men's roomy athletic socks
are the perfect size and thickness to shield dainty
pumps from scuffs and scratches when they're packed
in a suitcase. What's more, the socks will prevent any
dirt from transferring to your clothes.

how to hand wash delicates

1   2   3   4

PICK A GENTLE DETERGENT
Be sure to use a product made specifically for delicates. Unlike regular laundry detergents, which contain tough grease- and dirt-fighting ingredients that render them alkaline or acidic, detergents for delicates are closer to a neutral pH, and thus kinder on both fragile fabrics and your hands. These include Woolite—which offers good results and great value— as well as fancier formulas.

SWIRL, DIP, AND TWIRL
Fill a basin with warm water (about 85° F—just warm to the touch) and add a small amount of your detergent (a teaspoon should be enough). Disperse the soap by swirling your hand in the water. Put the garment in and twirl it around in a circular motion. Don't pull or stretch the fabric, or rub it against itself— these actions can change the garment's shape.

RINSE THOROUGHLY
After twirling the garment for two to five minutes, drain the water. Fold the garment over onto itself and gently press it against the side of the basin to squeeze out excess water. Refill the basin with clean warm water and repeat the twirling-and-draining cycle. Do this repeatedly until suds and slickness are gone. Avoid rinsing the garment under running water, which can stretch it out.

DRY AND SHAPE
Lay the garment on a white towel and smooth out any wrinkles. (Before doing this, you can extract even more water with a salad spinner; see page 42.) Roll up the towel with the garment in it, and press down to make the towel absorb the water. Unroll and repeat with a dry towel if the garment is still dripping wet. Finally, place the garment on a drying rack and arrange it to match its original shape.

1

2

3

4

fabric-softener sheets

THREAD DETANGLER
To stop thread from twisting and knotting up, run the threaded needle through a fabric-softener sheet before starting to sew.

BOOK DEODORIZER
Prevent your beloved old volumes from acquiring a musty smell by inserting a fabric-softener sheet between the pages.

SHOE FRESHENER
Sadly, shoes don't keep that just-purchased scent past one or two wearings. Place rolled-up sheets in the toes to control odor.

◄ DRAWER SCENTER
If fabric-softener sheets make your clothes smell nice in the dryer, just think what they could do in your dresser. Slip a few fresh ones between folded clothes.

SAWDUST CLEARER
For wiping up sawdust after drilling, you need something that can grab the fine particles. A used fabric-softener sheet will do the trick.

SCUM BUSTER
Remove obstinate soap buildup from glass shower doors by sprinkling a few drops of water onto a used fabric-softener sheet and scrubbing.

CLING COMBATANT
When static attacks, pat yourself down with a fabric-softener sheet to get rid of the electricity.

in the kitchen

Ah, the kitchen…gathering place, homework space, hub of the household. Amid all this activity, how do you manage to prepare actual meals? By having everything you need at your fingertips: the requisite skill sets, key ingredients, and essential tools (or surprisingly effective pinch hitters). Your reward? Less time spent cooking—and more time to dish.

pantry staples

ONIONS AND GARLIC ....

Look for ones with very dry and papery skins, because they'll keep the longest (up to two months).

HERBS AND SPICES ....

The most versatile flavors to have on hand are black pepper, paprika, oregano, fennel, and ground cumin. Buy spices in small containers so you use them up before the flavor fades (about four to six months). And don't forget kosher or sea salt.

TUNA ....

Whether packed in water or oil, canned tuna is great for making sandwiches, of course, but it's also a healthy addition to green salads and pasta dishes.

TOMATOES ....

Opt for cans of whole tomatoes (not crushed or pureed), since they contain the highest-quality tomatoes—and it doesn't take long to dice them yourself.

PASTA AND RICE ....

To cover the majority of recipes and dishes, store a few varieties, like linguine, penne, and lasagna noodles, and wild, brown, and basmati rice.

BEANS ....

Have a stash of white (cannellini, navy, garbanzo), pink or red (kidney, pinto), and black beans for salads, soups, and sides.

CORNMEAL

This is a key ingredient for muffins, breading, and, of course, corn bread.

HONEY

Drop a spoonful into plain yogurt or hot tea, or use it to make glazes, salad dressings, or desserts.

BREADCRUMBS

The freshly made kind may taste better, but the store-bought versions last longer—up to six months if unopened.

CHICKEN BROTH

Purchase it in either cans or cartons (both of which must be refrigerated after opening).

NUTS

Not only are they baking stars, but nuts like almonds, pecans, walnuts, and peanuts are delicious in salads and perfect for healthy snacking.

BAKING SUPPLIES

Stock everything you need to satisfy a sweet tooth: sugar, brown sugar, confectioners' sugar, cocoa, flour, baking powder, baking soda, yeast, cornstarch, shortening, vanilla extract, and semisweet chocolate chips.

OILS AND VINEGARS

Choose canola oil when you don't want to add flavor and extra-virgin olive oil when you do. Have red, white, and balsamic vinegars at the ready for preparing salad dressings and marinades.

for breakfast

FRESH TAKE ON FRUIT

A morning bowlful of raspberries can be a bit predictable and one-dimensional. Try drizzling a tablespoon of balsamic vinegar over the top for a more tart— and tempting—option.

PORTABLE PROTEIN

Skip the sweet syrup with your frozen toaster waffle. Instead, go for something savory that will curb your hunger until lunch: a slathering of peanut butter, a sprinkling of raisins, and some sesame seeds for an extra shot of fiber.

FAR-FROM-PLAIN YOGURT

Add whole-berry cranberry sauce, tangerine or clementine sections, and chopped pistachios to unflavored yogurt to supply your daily dose of calcium with tang and crunch.

GOURMET OATMEAL ▶

Oatmeal's closest cousins are porridge, gruel, and mush. Snooze. To perk up this ho-hum but heart-healthy hot cereal, cook it with skim or whole milk, then stir in apple chunks, maple syrup, and chopped cashews.

for lunch

GRILLED CHEESE GONE GREEK

Make your grilled-cheese sandwich into an exotic Mediterranean meal by layering Feta, sun-dried tomatoes, and olive tapenade in a pita pocket and placing it on a hot oiled skillet until the cheese starts to soften.

SOUPED-UP SOUP

Revive tired tomato bisque by dropping in dried wasabi peas and Goldfish crackers. Another idea: Stir shredded fresh spinach into the soup just before serving, then finish with a dollop of sour cream and orange zest.

THE CONDIMENT, RETHOUGHT

For an extra kick of flavor in your sandwich, substitute hummus for mayonnaise. Like mayo, hummus adds moisture, but it also offers a good dose of protein and a more palatable texture.

◄ **THIRTY-SECOND SALAD**

Spoon a little olive-oil-and-vinegar dressing into a halved (and pitted) avocado, then eat the savory fruit straight out of the skin.

for dinner and dessert

FAKING HOMEMADE

Haven't got the time or the inclination to make those peanut-butter thumbprints? Pop store-made cookies (the ones in the grocery bakery section) in the microwave for about 30 seconds to give them a soft, home-baked quality. Serve immediately.

BURGER HEAVEN

Ketchup and mustard can go only so far. To truly transform your burger, doctor the ground beef beforehand by mixing in your favorite marinade or sauce. The result? A tastier, juicier creation.

DESSERT SPREAD

There's no reason crostini should be limited to the hors d'oeuvres tray. Top toasted baguette slices with mascarpone cheese, berries, and a few drops of honey for a surprising sweet treat.

NEW-AND-IMPROVED SPAGHETTI NIGHT ▶

Spice up standard supermarket tomato sauce (and the standard Sunday-night supper) by swirling in store-bought pesto before you toss it with hot pasta.

master grocery list

Post a copy of this comprehensive shopping list—which is grouped by aisle and ordered according to the typical supermarket setup—in your kitchen, and check off items when you run out of them. That way, you'll be prepared for every grocery-store excursion (and never forget the milk again).

PRODUCE/DELI
- ☐ Lemons
- ☐ Limes
- ☐ Apples
- ☐ Bananas
- ☐ Grapes
- ☐ Pears
- ☐ Berries
- ☐ Grapefruit
- ☐ Other fruits:

_____
_____

- ☐ Celery
- ☐ Tomatoes
- ☐ Lettuce
- ☐ Prewashed salad
- ☐ Bell peppers
- ☐ Carrots
- ☐ Onions
- ☐ Scallions
- ☐ Garlic
- ☐ Potatoes
- ☐ Green beans
- ☐ Corn
- ☐ Spinach
- ☐ Avocados
- ☐ Cucumbers
- ☐ Asparagus

- ☐ Mushrooms
- ☐ Broccoli
- ☐ Cauliflower
- ☐ Other vegetables:

_____
_____
_____

- ☐ Fresh herbs
- ☐ Deli meats
- ☐ Deli cheese

MEAT/FISH
- ☐ Beef
- ☐ Chicken
- ☐ Turkey
- ☐ Pork
- ☐ Sausage
- ☐ Seafood

DRY GOODS
- ☐ Bread
- ☐ Cereal
- ☐ Breadcrumbs
- ☐ Oatmeal
- ☐ Crackers
- ☐ Chips
- ☐ Pretzels
- ☐ Cookies
- ☐ Granola bars
- ☐ Popcorn

- ☐ Pasta
- ☐ Beans
- ☐ Rice
- ☐ Other dry goods:

_____
_____
_____

BAKING GOODS
- ☐ Sugar
- ☐ Confectioners' sugar
- ☐ Brown sugar
- ☐ Honey
- ☐ Flour
- ☐ Baking soda
- ☐ Baking powder
- ☐ Cornstarch
- ☐ Chocolate chips
- ☐ Raisins
- ☐ Cake mix
- ☐ Pancake mix
- ☐ Cocoa
- ☐ Marshmallows
- ☐ Cornmeal
- ☐ Shortening
- ☐ Yeast
- ☐ Salt
- ☐ Pepper
- ☐ Extracts

- ☐ Dried herbs
- ☐ Dried spices
- ☐ Nuts
- ☐ Other baking goods:

_____
_____

CANNED/JARRED GOODS
- ☐ Tomatoes
- ☐ Tomato paste
- ☐ Tomato sauce
- ☐ Fruit
- ☐ Applesauce
- ☐ Tuna
- ☐ Broth
- ☐ Bouillon
- ☐ Soup
- ☐ Other canned/ jarred goods:

_____
_____

CONDIMENTS/ SAUCES
- ☐ Oil
- ☐ Vinegar
- ☐ Mayonnaise

- ☐ Ketchup
- ☐ Mustard
- ☐ Relish
- ☐ Peanut butter
- ☐ Jelly/jam
- ☐ Salad dressing
- ☐ Soy sauce
- ☐ Salsa
- ☐ Pickles
- ☐ Other condiments/ sauces:

_____
_____

BEVERAGES (NONCHILLED)
- ☐ Soda
- ☐ Seltzer
- ☐ Juice
- ☐ Water
- ☐ Tea
- ☐ Coffee
- ☐ Coffee filters
- ☐ Beer
- ☐ Wine
- ☐ Other beverages:

_____
_____

FROZEN
- ☐ Ice cream
- ☐ Pizza
- ☐ Waffles
- ☐ Vegetables
- ☐ Dinners
- ☐ Juice
- ☐ Other frozen items:

_____
_____

DAIRY
- ☐ Skim milk
- ☐ Whole milk
- ☐ Eggs
- ☐ Cream
- ☐ Sour cream
- ☐ Cottage cheese
- ☐ Cream cheese
- ☐ Butter
- ☐ Buttermilk
- ☐ Yogurt—plain
- ☐ Yogurt—flavored
- ☐ Orange juice
- ☐ Cheese
- ☐ Other dairy:

_____
_____

For a tear-out version of this crib sheet, see the booklet on the inside back cover.

cooking and baking substitutes

IF YOU DON'T HAVE	USE	IF YOU DON'T HAVE	USE
1 tablespoon baking powder	$^1/_4$ teaspoon baking soda, plus $^5/_8$ teaspoon cream of tartar	1 egg	$^1/_4$ cup egg substitute (such as Egg Beaters)
1 cup granulated sugar	$1^3/_4$ cups powdered sugar	1 teaspoon lemon juice	$^1/_2$ teaspoon white vinegar
1 ounce unsweetened baking chocolate	3 tablespoons unsweetened cocoa, plus 1 tablespoon melted butter	1 small onion	$^1/_2$ tablespoon onion powder
1 ounce bittersweet chocolate	1 ounce semisweet chocolate	1 clove garlic	$^1/_2$ teaspoon garlic salt or $^1/_8$ teaspoon garlic powder
1 tablespoon cornstarch	2 tablespoons all-purpose flour (for thickening only)	1 cup ketchup	1 cup jarred tomato sauce, plus 4 tablespoons sugar and 2 tablespoons white vinegar
1 cup light corn syrup	$1^1/_4$ cups granulated sugar, plus $^1/_4$ cup water; boil to dissolve sugar	1 jalapeño pepper	$^1/_4$ teaspoon red pepper flakes
1 cup honey	$1^1/_4$ cups granulated sugar, plus $^1/_3$ cup liquid used in recipe (e.g., milk); boil to dissolve sugar	1 cup broth (chicken or beef)	1 bouillon cube (and omit any additional salt from recipe)
		1 tablespoon fresh herbs	1 teaspoon dried herbs
1 cup whole milk	1 cup skim milk, plus 2 tablespoons melted butter	1 cup fresh berries	8 ounces frozen berries
		1 cup white wine	1 cup dry vermouth
1 cup sour cream	$^3/_4$ cup plain whole yogurt, plus $^1/_3$ cup melted butter	1 cup red wine	1 cup grape or cranberry juice, plus 1 tablespoon white vinegar
1 cup buttermilk or yogurt	1 cup milk, plus 1 tablespoon lemon juice	Mozzarella	Italian Fontina
		Parmigiano-Reggiano	Pecorino or Asiago
1 cup butter	$^7/_8$ cup vegetable oil or 1 cup shortening	Ricotta	Cottage cheese
1 cup mayonnaise	1 cup whole sour cream or yogurt	Stilton	Gorgonzola or Roquefort

MEASUREMENT EQUIVALENTS

Pinch or dash = $^1/_{16}$ teaspoon	1 tablespoon = $^1/_{16}$ cup = $^1/_2$ fluid ounce	1 quart = 2 pints = 32 fluid ounces
3 teaspoons = 1 tablespoon	1 cup = 16 tablespoons = 8 fluid ounces	1 gallon = 4 quarts = 128 fluid ounces
	1 pint = 2 cups = 16 fluid ounces	16 ounces = 1 pound

scissors

OLD USE: Paper cutter.

NEW USE: Pizza slicer. A pair of scissors will cut through the dough in one pass (no more going back and forth repeatedly). Scissors also come in handy when precut delivery pizza won't separate into neat wedges.

salt

OLD USE: Pretzel topper.

NEW USE: Grit remover. To make washing dirt-trapping leafy greens like spinach easier, swirl them in a bath of salt water. The salt's abrasiveness helps scrub the surfaces of the leaves.

wine bottle

OLD USE: Syrah holder.

NEW USE: Dough shaper. When you need to flatten dough and your rolling pin is nowhere to be found, a wine bottle will do the trick (place a sheet of plastic wrap between the bottle and dough to avoid sticking). If the bottle is empty, you can fill it with ice-cold water and cork it to keep the dough chilled.

fork

OLD USE: Food transporter.

NEW USE: Flow regulator. Use a fork's tines to poke small holes in the foil seals of oil, syrup, and salad-dressing bottles. That way, you'll prevent the liquids from gushing.

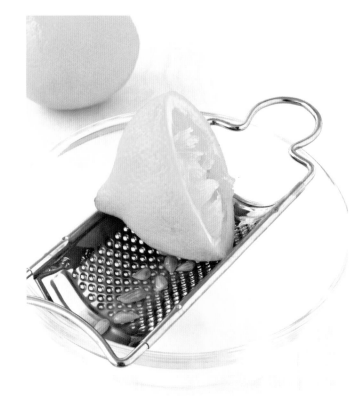

cheese grater

OLD USE: Taco-making tool.

NEW USE: Lemon-juice strainer. Squeeze the citrus fruit over the grater and into a bowl—the juice will flow through, but the seeds and the pulp will remain on top for easy disposal.

aluminum foil

OLD USE: Cover for leftovers.

NEW USE: Pan-in-a-pinch. Rather than struggling to dislodge your rustic apple masterpiece from its (supposedly) nonstick pan, bake it on a cookie sheet, supporting its sides with a doubled-over strip of foil. Secure the foil with a paper clip.

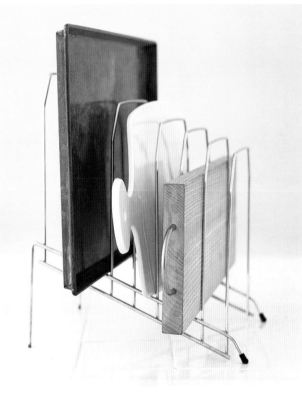

newspaper

OLD USE: Reading material.

NEW USE: Tomato ripener. To help prematurely picked tomatoes come to fruition faster, wrap them individually in newspaper (and leave them out at room temperature) to trap the ethylene they emit.

file rack

OLD USE: Folder displayer.

NEW USE: Cookie-sheet and cutting-board organizer. Relocate your rack from the office to the kitchen and use it to contain those big, flat items. Store the rack in your cupboard and take advantage of all that underused vertical space.

how to slice anything

1 2 3

AVOCADO
(ALSO WORKS FOR PAPAYAS)

A. Using a chef's knife, halve the avocado lengthwise, then twist the two halves apart.

B. To remove the pit, hold the avocado firmly in one hand and whack the knife into the pit. Do this with conviction, so the knife lodges firmly. Then twist the knife to pull the pit out.

C. With the tip of a paring knife, score the flesh, then scoop it out with a spoon. The avocado will emerge from the skin already diced for salads or guacamole.

ONION
(ALSO WORKS FOR SHALLOTS)

A. Peel the onion, leaving the root end intact. Using a chef's knife, take a small slice off the top, then halve the onion lengthwise. Lay one half cut-side down on a cutting board and make two or three horizontal cuts. Don't go all the way through; that way, the root end will remain intact.

B. Depending on the size of the onion, make 5 to 10 evenly spaced vertical cuts, leaving the root end intact.

C. Now, for the perfect dice, rotate the onion 90 degrees and make a series of slices downward (toward the cutting board) all the way through. The closer the slices, the finer the dice.

ORANGE
(ALSO WORKS FOR GRAPEFRUIT)

A. Trim both ends of the fruit for stability. Use a chef's knife to cut away the skin and pith (the bitter white part), following the natural curve of the fruit.

B. Working over a bowl to catch the juice, carefully cut along each side of the membrane to free each section from the core.

C. Squeeze the membranes to extract the remaining juice.

1A

1B

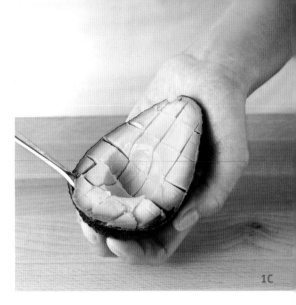

1C

2A

2B

2C

3A

3B

3C

4A

4B

4C

5A

5B

5C

6A

6B

6C

how to slice anything

BASIL
(ALSO WORKS FOR MINT)

A. Stack the leaves in a pile, placing the larger leaves on the bottom and the smaller ones on top.

B. Roll the pile lengthwise as tightly as possible. Then, using a chef's or paring knife, slice across the bundle. The closer the slices, the thinner the shreds will be.

C. Fluff and separate the shreds with your fingertips.

OLIVE
(STEPS A AND B ALSO WORK TO REMOVE THE SKIN FROM GARLIC CLOVES)

A. Using your fist or the heel of your hand, smash the olive under the flat side of a chef's knife to break the skin.

B. Take the olive in your hand and twist the skin to further loosen the pit.

C. Remove the exposed pit, then chop the olive with a chef's or paring knife.

JALAPEÑO
(ALSO WORKS FOR BELL PEPPERS)

A. Using a paring knife, and standing the jalapeño up by holding its stem, slice its flesh into four "fillets."

B. Most of the jalapeño's heat is found in the now exposed core that holds the seeds. If you want extra heat, save and chop some of the core and seeds.

C. Slice the jalapeño fillets into strips, then crosswise into a fine dice.

vinegar

EGG STAINER
Distinguishing between raw and hard-boiled can be easy if you boil eggs with a few drops of balsamic vinegar to tint the shells slightly.

LEATHER CLEANER
Erase salt stains from leather shoes or boots by treating them with a solution of equal parts vinegar and water, using a soft cloth or brush.

TAG DISLODGER
Remove a gummy sticker by dampening it with vinegar. Let it sit for five minutes, then rub it off with a cotton ball or a paper towel.

◄ **ODOR REMOVER**
After chopping onions, scrub your hands with salt and a splash of vinegar to eliminate the smell.

BATH IMPROVER
Add $1/2$ cup of vinegar to the water to soothe dry skin—and get a cleaner bathtub. Essential oil can help counteract the scent.

DISPOSAL SANITIZER
Disinfect and deodorize a garbage disposal by making vinegar ice cubes, grinding them up, and rinsing with cold water.

COFFEEMAKER CLEARER
To get rid of buildup, fill the carafe with a solution of one part vinegar to three parts water and run the brew cycle. Then run a few cycles of water.

in the office

Every Monday morning, your mind inevitably drifts to some far-off place: Fiji, perhaps? But if you streamline your duties and spruce up your surroundings, you won't feel that pressing need to escape the workaday here and now. Added benefit: When it *does* come time for that trip to Fiji, you'll know exactly where to find your frequent-flier number.

desk-drawer essentials

ANTIPERSPIRANT ....
Keep a travel-size deodorant and antiper-spirant handy to provide an added layer of protection on hot or stressful days.

EYEDROPS ....
Bone-dry office air and hours spent in front of a computer can leave eyes irritated. Saline drops help restore moisture.

TAMPONS ....
It's smart to store a spare or two—the vending machine at work is empty most of the time, anyway.

FIRST-AID SUPPLIES ....
Annoying paper cuts and pinkie-toe blisters necessitate bandages in various sizes. And acetaminophen (or ibuprofen or aspirin) should do the trick for minor aches and pains.

SAFETY PINS ....
When you don't have the time or the supplies to fix a fallen hem or sew on a button, a safety pin can act as a stand-in.

MINI LINT ROLLER ....
To remove lint and hair from your clothing, do a quick rollover before important meetings or heading out the door.

ANTIBACTERIAL MOIST TOWELETTES ....
For pre- and post-meal washups, disinfecting a germ-covered phone, and cleaning up sticky spills, antibacterial wipes are indispensable. Opt for the individually wrapped ones; they won't dry out and are small enough to stash anywhere.

BREATH MINTS ....
Pop one in your mouth after you finish your morning coffee.

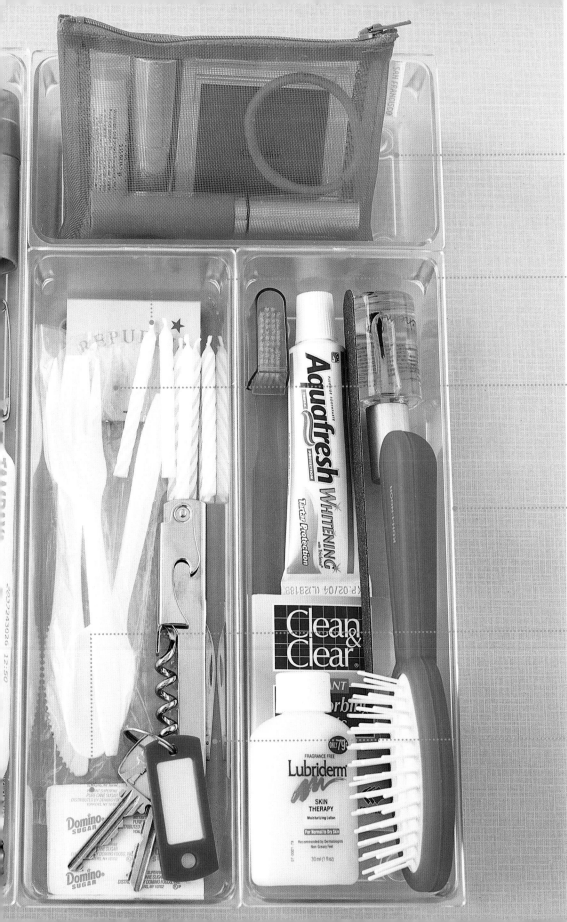

TOUCH-UP ITEMS

Instead of schlepping your makeup bag between home and the office, tuck a few must-haves in a zippered pouch and let them live in your desk: concealer, blush, lip balm, lipstick, and a hair elastic.

PARTY STAPLES

With candles, matches, and a corkscrew, you'll be fully prepared for those impromptu coworker birthday celebrations and Champagne toasts in the hallway.

PLASTIC UTENSILS

Rather than scrounging for silverware every time you eat lunch at your desk, put plastic versions in your drawer. Restock with the extras from take-out deliveries or leftovers from staff functions.

GROOMING SUPPLIES

A few drugstore items—toothbrush and toothpaste, nail file, clear nail polish, brush, lotion, and blotting papers—can go a long way in helping you look put-together all day.

SUGAR PACKETS

You're probably not the only one adding sweetener to her morning cup of coffee, so for those days when your office kitchen runs out of packets, keep a few here.

SPARE HOUSE KEYS

Along with the set at your neighbor's, drop a set of house keys into your drawer for emergencies, but don't label them, for security's sake.

for your desk

PERSONAL PAPERWEIGHT

Instead of a generic glass or metal disk, pick one of your favorite mementos— a shell or rock from last summer or a piece of your child's pottery—to keep piles of paper neat.

A LIVELY ADDITION

Nothing brightens up a gloomy office like a potted plant. Go with a hardy variety that can withstand the dry air and doesn't need daily waterings, such as aloe vera (shown above) or another type of succulent.

NEW STASH OF SCRAP PAPER

Stack outdated business cards in a small bowl next to your phone, and use them as scrap paper. Their sturdy stock and petite size make them perfect for scribbling down phone numbers and notes to self.

A SOFTER SEAT ▶

Placing a colorful pillow on your desk chair helps to make it feel more comfortable—and look more cheerful. Choose one about the same size as the back of your seat that's cushioned enough to give you lumbar support.

for your workspace

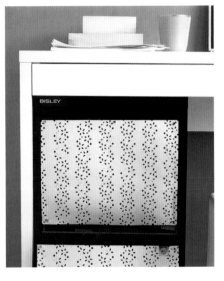

PRETTIER POSTINGS

Your plain old bulletin board will look more like wall art if you paint its frame and, alongside the usual contact lists, add photos, note cards, and souvenirs from vacations (think starfish).

FILING-CABINET REFURBISHMENT

Corporate black or gray cabinets leave much to be desired…color being at the top of the list. So dress up the fronts of the drawers with sheets of wallpaper or wrapping paper—just cut them to size and secure them with mini magnets.

STRESS-REDUCING SCENT

Hang a sachet over the inside doorknob of your office and you'll replace the fragrance of industrial carpeting and recirculated air with that of a lavender field or a rose garden.

◄ OFFICE BLACKBOARD

Desperate for a place to put your big ideas or your do-or-die to-do list? Try the wall. Paint a section with chalkboard paint (sold at art-supply and hardware stores) and your important memos can be writ large.

vital deskside information

TRAVEL	FINANCES	WHAT PAPERS TO KEEP—AND FOR HOW LONG
AIRLINES	**CREDIT CARDS**	**KEEP FOR ONE MONTH**
Airline:	Type of credit card:	■ Credit-card receipts
Phone number:	Phone number:	■ Receipts for minor purchases
Frequent-flier number:		■ Withdrawal and deposit slips; toss after you've checked them against your monthly bank statement
Airline:	Type of credit card:	
Phone number:	Phone number:	
Frequent-flier number:		**KEEP FOR ONE YEAR**
	Type of credit card:	■ Paycheck stubs
Airline:	Phone number:	■ Monthly bank, credit-card, brokerage, mutual-fund, and retirement-account statements
Phone number:		
Frequent-flier number:	Type of credit card:	
	Phone number:	**KEEP FOR SIX YEARS**
Airline:		■ W-2s, 1099s, and the other guts of your tax returns
Phone number:	**BANKS AND BENEFITS**	■ Year-end credit-card, brokerage, and mutual-fund statements
Frequent-flier number:	Bank:	
	Phone number:	**KEEP INDEFINITELY**
RENTAL CARS		■ Tax returns
Rental-car company:	Bank:	■ Receipts for major purchases
Phone number:	Phone number:	■ Real-estate and residence records
Frequent-renter number:		■ Birth and death certificates
	Benefits contact:	■ Marriage licenses
Rental-car company:	Phone number:	
Phone number:		**KEEP IN A SAFE-DEPOSIT BOX**
Frequent-renter number:	Retirement-savings contact:	■ Insurance policies
	Phone number:	■ Wills and trusts
		■ Deed(s) to your home(s)
	Health-insurance contact:	
	Phone number:	

For a tear-out version of this crib sheet, see the booklet on the inside back cover.

vital deskside information

SHIPPING AND MAILING

FEDEX

Phone number:

Account number:

Drop-off location:

UPS

Phone number:

Account number:

Drop-off location:

DHL

Phone number:

Account number:

Drop-off location:

USPS

Local branch phone number:

Local branch location:

OTHER SERVICES

PHONE

Company name:

Company phone number:

Service plan:

FAX

Brand and model:

Manufacturer phone number:

COMPUTER AND PRINTER

Computer technician:

Phone number:

Computer serial number:

Computer brand and model:

Printer brand and model:

INTERNET PROVIDER

Provider name:

Phone number:

Service plan:

PDA

Brand and model:

Manufacturer phone number:

CREATING A PAPER-FILING SYSTEM

Now that you know what documents to keep (see page 80), here's how to keep them.

■ A file cabinet is ideal, but if space is at a premium, use a file box that slips underneath a desk or fits on a bookshelf.

■ Write out a list of the types of statements you get each month (and every two months, and twice a year). As you do, categories for filing will suggest themselves. The key is to find a naming system that meets your needs and triggers your memory.

■ Once you've determined your categories, organize them by broad subject (say, medical), then by subsubject (health coverage, dental coverage, etc.).

■ Each tax season, go through your file and toss what's no longer needed.

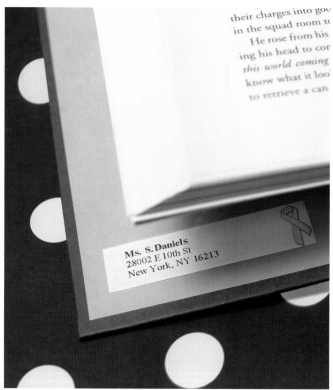

spring

OLD USE: Pinball projector.

NEW USE: Mail sorter. A heavy-gauge spring (sold at hardware stores) can act as a horizontal file to keep your invitations and RSVP cards upright and visible.

return-address label

OLD USE: Letter-writing time-saver.

NEW USE: Property identifier. Stick or tape one to anything you might lend but don't want to lose— your books, CDs, food containers, etc. The borrower can't help but remember where to return the item when she is finished with it.

185

: other day," my mom said, spinning around.
:?" My father had been a PC guy since the days
ly computers that existed. He learned how to
ter the size of a wall. His favorite pastime was
baqs and putting the hard drives in new ones.
it he had thirty half-dismantled computers
ce.
ie to make the switch," he said. "I want to get
ig and the graphics programs work so much
iised the box and ran his finger over the pic-
:?"
!" I said. "When I told you I was using one in
esleyan you didn't speak to me for a week."
was antiquated and stubborn, which I have
pletely true. Macs are the way of the future."
onger than a million "Switch" commercials.
oull an entire ship.
r see how unusual he was acting? A PC-to-Mac
of of infidelity than lipstick on the collar.

twist tie

OLD USE: Trash-bag tamer.

NEW USE: Wire gatherer. If the cords streaming from your lamp, computer, and phone are in complete, well, discord, cinch them together with a twist tie.

bobby pin

OLD USE: Bun securer.

NEW USE: Bookmark. Want a sturdier (and cuter) alternative to the typical yellow Post-it note? Use a bobby pin to flag a frequently turned-to section in a reference book or to mark your place in a novel (slide the pin over a few pages so it stays put).

file-folder labels

OLD USE: Favorite tools of type As.

NEW USE: Cord labelers. Attach adhesive file-folder labels with the names of the cords' owners (for example, phone, computer, fax, and lamp; or TV, DVD, VCR, and phone) near the plugs. This way you can quickly ID which cord belongs to which machine— and you won't unplug the wrong one.

emery board

OLD USE: Nail shaper.

NEW USE: Eraser CPR. To revive a dried-out eraser or clean a smudged one, lightly rub it over an emery board. The board's fine grain will shave off the eraser's old top layer, leaving you with a good-as-new mistake-removing surface.

napkin holder

OLD USE: Kitchen-countertop neatener.

NEW USE: Bill organizer. Instead of mounding your monthly invoices in a messy pile, repurpose a napkin holder to stash them in a more civilized manner. File bills in the order of their due dates to make your life even easier.

spice containers

OLD USE: Homes for cumin and cayenne.

NEW USE: Office-supply corralers. Use these squat, clear-topped jars (sold at kitchen-supply stores) to keep all those loose bits cluttering your desk drawer—stamps and Post-it notes, thumbtacks and rubber bands, safety pins and stickers—under control.

how to be most efficient

KNOW YOUR INTERNAL CLOCK

Schedule meetings, reviews, presentations, and other important events for when you're especially alert— most likely in the mid- to late morning, between 9 and 11 A.M. To find out what your natural pattern is, record a log for a few days, charting your energy level every hour on a scale from 1 to 10.

SET UP MAIL-TAMING SYSTEMS

■ For snail mail: Only touch it once, at a specific time each day (perhaps right after lunch or right before you leave work). File what you need and trash the rest.
■ For e-mail: Delete anything you don't have to save as soon as you read it. And set up folders in your e-mail program—both work-related (sales meeting, future projects) and personal (travel plans, book group)—to organize saved messages. If you need to respond to certain e-mails but don't have time to do so right away, flag them. Then designate the same time each day to replying to them.

SNACK REGULARLY

Keep nuts or dried fruit handy to munch on when you hit your lowest energy levels, usually between 3 and 5 P.M. For variety, mix them up; healthy combinations include pineapple and pistachios, almonds and apricots, raisins and peanuts, and cherries and hazelnuts. A handful is all you'll need to get a fast— and lasting—energy boost.

DON'T MULTITASK!

Studies have shown that if you tackle two things simultaneously (say, talking on the phone and answering e-mail), you'll end up doing each less effectively— and take longer to do them. Instead, devote discrete chunks of time to individual tasks, and focus on each solely and completely.

1

2

3

4

WEDNESDAY | THURSDAY

MARCH
S	M	T	W	T	F	S
		1	2	3	4	5
6	7	8	9	10	11	12
13	14	15	16	17	18	19
20	21	22	23	24	25	26
27	28	29	30	31		

MAY
S	M	T	W	T	F	S
1	2	3	4	5	6	7
8	9	10	11	12	13	14
15	16	17	18	19	20	21
22	23	24	25	26	27	28
29	30	31				

SUNDAY	MONDAY	TUESDAY		
3	4	5	6	7
Daylight Saving Time begins				
10	11	12	13	14
National Library Week begins				
17	18	19	20	21
24	25	26	27	28

velcro

PICTURE HANGER
To display art without nailing holes, attach several wide strips of adhesive-backed Velcro to the wall and to the back of a lightweight frame.

TOY SUSPENDER
Affix a wide strip of adhesive-backed Velcro (the hook side) to a wall, then sew small pieces (the loop side) to stuffed animals.

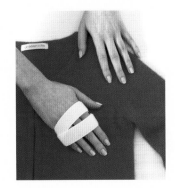

SWEATER SMOOTHER
Lightly glide a piece of Velcro (the hook side) over a sweater to grab offending pills.

◀ **PEN MINDER**
Velcro a pen next to your wall calendar so you can scribble in birthdays and appointments (no more scrambling to find a writing instrument).

BLOUSE SECURER
Prevent your button-down shirt from gaping open by sewing or sticking two small pieces of Velcro between the buttons.

CUSHION KEEPER
Stop a seat cushion from tumbling off a chair by adhering strips of Velcro to the bottom of the cushion and the top of the seat.

REMOTE CONTROLLER
Place the hook side of a piece of Velcro on the TV, then the corresponding loop side on the back of the remote.

cleaning

Until the self-cleaning household becomes a reality, you, alas, must rely on more conventional tidying-up techniques. Thankfully, getting every room spick-and-span doesn't have to call for your entire supply of elbow grease. When you have the proper systems and tools at your disposal, your house will essentially clean itself. Well, almost.

dishwasher fundamentals

DURABLE GLASSES AND MUGS ....

Place sturdy glassware and mugs between
the top rack's prongs—that way, the water
jets will have a clear shot into each glass.

PLATES AND BOWLS ....

Make sure soiled dish surfaces face
the center of the dishwasher—not the
outside—so they'll get a full blast of water.
To keep smaller items from being sand-
wiched between two larger ones (and not
getting cleaned), group same-size bowls
and plates together when possible.

FLATWARE ....

Mix up your utensils so spoons don't nest
with spoons and forks with forks. Stick
knives in the basket blade-side down to
avoid dishwasher-emptying injuries.

..... POTS AND PANS

Load large dishes, pots, and pans on the top rack so they won't block the spray arm and prevent water from reaching the rest of the load. Reminder: You'll need to hand wash cast-iron and anodized cookware, plus anything made of wood or pewter, gold flatware, glassware that's especially breakable, and high-quality knives.

..... FRAGILE GLASSES

Position delicate and/or tipsy dishwasher-safe glassware over the top rack's prongs to keep it upright and stabilized.

..... SURPRISING ITEMS

A dishwasher is an equal-opportunity appliance—it doesn't clean dining- and cookware alone. So what else can you stick in there? Try plastic hairbrushes and combs, sponges, dish racks, plastic toys, burner knobs and grates, drain catchers, refrigerator drawers and shelves, toothbrushes, shower caddies, soap dishes, and the filter from the stove's exhaust hood.

for tools

MILDER SUBSTITUTE

Use hydrogen peroxide to clean the bathroom. Not only is it effective at killing germs but the fumes won't leave you as light-headed as other cleaning supplies' fumes do.

DIRT-GRABBING DOORMAT

What's the best way to keep your house cleaner longer? Stop dirt at the door with a mat made of AstroTurf or another toothed material. The teeth truly trap debris—unlike other matting materials, which leave dirt on the surface to get tracked in by the next person.

CAR-WASH CONCEPT

To prevent soap scum, mildew, and hard-water stains from forming in the shower—and to save yourself from having to scrub them off—use a squee-gee to wipe down the walls and the glass door (with or without the help of a cleaning solution) after you bathe.

MULTITASKING CLOTH ▶

Rather than switching between sponges and rags when you clean and dust, let microfiber cloths do it all. They attract and hold dirt, don't require any cleaning agents (only a bit of water), and can be machine washed.

for methods

SHINY SINK SOLUTION

To make your white sink sparkle,
fill the basin to the rim with very hot
water, add one cup of regular bleach
or hydrogen peroxide, and let sit for one
hour. Drain and rinse the basin, then
scrub it with a nonabrasive cleanser or
baking soda. Finally, rinse the basin,
shine it with glass cleaner, and dry.

EASY GREASE REMOVAL

Instead of soaking a dirty pan overnight,
get rid of baked-on grease this way: Fill
the pan halfway with water, add about a
tablespoon of baking soda, and bring to
a boil. Then remove the pan from the heat
and drop in a tablespoon of liquid dish
soap. Allow the solution to cool, then pour
it out. The grease should go with it.

FASTER RINSING

Use a spray bottle containing clean water
to rinse off the places you've washed.
It is simpler than rinsing a sponge and
going over the surface repeatedly, and it
will prevent soapy film, which can attract
dirt, from forming.

◀ DRIP CATCHER

When you're cleaning high places, fold
the edges of your rubber gloves up to
prevent cleanser from streaming down
your arms and soaking your sleeves.

stain-removal guide

OUTDOOR STAINS	BEVERAGE STAINS	STAIN-FIGHTERS GLOSSARY

ABSORBENTS: Cornstarch, talcum powder
WORK ON: Grease, oil

BLEACHES: White vinegar, ammonia, lemon juice
WORK ON: Color that remains after a stain treatment

COMBINATION SOLVENTS: Shout, Spray 'n Wash
WORK ON: Grease, oil, food, makeup

DIGESTANTS: Enzyme treatments such as Biz, Era, and Wisk
WORK ON: Protein stains, such as blood and grass

GLYCERIN: A syrupy solvent sold at drugstores
WORKS ON: Barbecue sauce

MILD DETERGENTS: Woolite, Ivory Snow
WORK ON: Mild stains, removing stain treatments from fabrics

OIL SOLVENTS: Dry-cleaning fluids such as K2r and Carbona
WORK ON: Greasy, oily stains on dry fabrics

MUD

WASHABLES: Let dry, then carefully brush off as much as possible. Apply a mild detergent (see Stain-Fighters Glossary, right, for examples) and water. Rub to form suds, then rinse. Bleach any remaining color with diluted vinegar (see Dilution Ratios, right). Machine wash.

NONWASHABLES: Let dry, then carefully brush off as much as possible. Use an eyedropper to apply a solution of one tablespoon of dishwashing liquid and one cup of water. Rinse with cold water.

GRASS

WASHABLES: Treat the spot with a paste made from a powder digestant and water and let sit in a warm place (such as outside in the sun) for 30 minutes. Use an eyedropper with diluted ammonia or vinegar to bleach. Machine wash.

NONWASHABLES: Apply a combination solvent and let sit for 15 minutes. Use an eyedropper with diluted ammonia or vinegar to bleach. Thoroughly flush the spot with cool water.

COFFEE

WASHABLES: Use an eyedropper with diluted vinegar to bleach. Flush with water. If the coffee had milk in it, apply a digestant and water. Machine wash.

NONWASHABLES: Apply a detergent and very little water. Rub to form suds and rinse. If the coffee had milk in it, apply an oil solvent. Use an eyedropper with diluted vinegar to bleach. Rinse.

RED WINE

WASHABLES: Cover the stain with salt. Stretch the fabric over a bowl. From a height of one foot, pour boiling water over it. Machine wash.

NONWASHABLES: Apply an oil solvent, let dry, and remove any residue. Use an eyedropper with diluted vinegar to bleach. Flush with cool water.

TEA

WASHABLES: Stretch the fabric over a bowl. From a height of one foot, pour boiling water over it. Use an eyedropper with diluted lemon juice to bleach. Machine wash.

NONWASHABLES: Use an eyedropper with diluted lemon juice to bleach. Rinse.

DILUTION RATIOS

AMMONIA: 1 part ammonia, 2 parts water
LEMON JUICE: 1 part juice, 1 part water
VINEGAR: 1 part white vinegar, 1 part water

For a tear-out version of this crib sheet, see the booklet on the inside back cover.

stain-removal guide

FOOD STAINS

MUSTARD

WASHABLES: Use an eyedropper with diluted ammonia to bleach. Apply a combination solvent and let sit for 15 minutes. Machine wash.

NONWASHABLES: Use an eyedropper with diluted ammonia to bleach. Apply a combination solvent and let sit for 15 minutes. Thoroughly flush the spot with cool water.

KETCHUP

WASHABLES: Apply a combination solvent. Use an eyedropper with diluted vinegar to bleach. Machine wash.

NONWASHABLES: Same as for washables, but instead of washing, thoroughly flush the spot with cool water.

BARBECUE SAUCE

WASHABLES: Apply glycerin, then rinse with cool water. Apply a combination solvent and let sit for 15 minutes. Machine wash.

NONWASHABLES: Apply glycerin, then rinse with cold water. Treat with a mild detergent and very little water. Gently rub to form suds, then rinse with cold water.

CHOCOLATE (INCLUDING ICE CREAM)

WASHABLES: Treat with a solution of one tablespoon of digestant and two cups of water. Let stand for 20 minutes. Machine wash.

NONWASHABLES: Apply rubbing alcohol, let sit for 10 minutes, then rinse. Use a combination of water and mild detergent to clean any residue. Rinse with cool water.

CRANBERRY SAUCE

WASHABLES: Flush the area with cool water. Use an eyedropper to apply diluted vinegar; let sit for 10 minutes. Apply a combination solvent. Machine wash.

NONWASHABLES: Blot with cold water. Use an eyedropper to apply diluted vinegar. Follow with an application of mild detergent and water to clean any residue. Rinse with cool water.

OIL-BASED SALAD DRESSING

WASHABLES: Shake on an absorbent to sop up the oil. Pick or scrape off any excess and rinse with cool water. Then apply a combination solvent and let sit for 15 minutes. Machine wash.

NONWASHABLES: Shake on an absorbent to sop up the oil. Pick or scrape off any excess and let dry. Follow with an application of an oil solvent. Let dry and scrape off any remaining residue.

OTHER STAINS

LIPSTICK

WASHABLES: Apply an oil solvent, then let dry. Remove residue. Treat with liquid soap and a little water. Rub to form suds; rinse. Use an eyedropper with diluted ammonia to bleach. Machine wash.

NONWASHABLES: Same as for washables, but use diluted vinegar instead of ammonia and rinse.

WAX

WASHABLES: Freeze the wax, then scrape off all you can. Stretch the fabric over a bowl. From a height of one foot, pour boiling water over it.

NONWASHABLES: Freeze the wax, then scrape off all you can. Clean the residue with an oil solvent.

DRIED BLOOD

WASHABLES: Soak in salt water for a few hours. Rinse and treat with diluted ammonia to bleach. If the stain persists, apply a paste of a powder digestant and water and let sit in a warm place for 30 minutes. Machine wash.

NONWASHABLES: Dampen with cool salt water, then plain water. Use an eyedropper with diluted vinegar to bleach. Flush with cool water.

clothespin

OLD USE: Clothesline partner.

NEW USE: Vacuum-cord keeper. To prevent the cord from being sucked back in while you're vacuuming, clip a clothespin onto it close to the machine.

lint roller

OLD USE: Fuzz eliminator.

NEW USE: Lamp-shade duster. Supporting the inside of the shade with your free hand, run a lint roller up and down the outside to remove dirt.

newspaper

OLD USE: Daily informer.

NEW USE: Mirror and window washer. Newspapers deposit less lint than paper towels do and don't leave any streaks. Just spray on a glass cleaner and wipe.

denture tablets

OLD USE: False-teeth freshener.

NEW USE: Vase cleaner. When residue clings to unreachable spots inside a vase or decanter, fill the container with warm water and drop in one or two denture-cleaning tablets for every eight ounces of warm water. Let the fizzy solution sit for the time specified on the product's box, then rinse.

electric toothbrush

OLD USE: Smile polisher.

NEW USE: Tile scourer. Dip an old, retired toothbrush head into a solution of all-purpose cleanser and water, and use it to scrub tile grout, bathroom fixtures, and any other nook or cranny a larger brush can't reach.

terra-cotta pot

OLD USE: Plant home.

NEW USE: Garden-tool holder. Fill a terra-cotta pot with builder's sand (sold at hardware stores), then stir in some mineral oil—just enough to dampen the sand. The mixture will clean the tools and prevent corrosion and rust. (If the pot has a hole on the bottom, cover it with duct tape.)

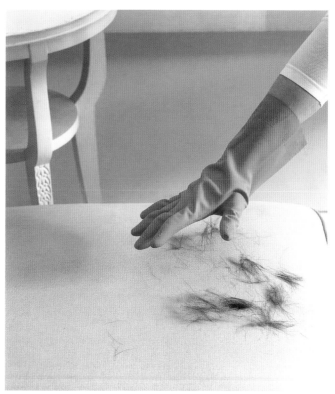

cotton swabs

OLD USE: Makeup implements.

NEW USE: Computer detailers. With the machine turned off, disconnect the keyboard and trace between the keys with a cotton swab lightly dipped in isopropyl alcohol. If your mouse is the kind that rolls on a ball, unscrew the bottom and go over the ball and the interior with a cotton swab, too.

rubber glove

OLD USE: Dishwashing assistant.

NEW USE: Pet-hair remover. Put on a damp rubber dishwashing glove and run your hand over hair-covered upholstery—the hair will cling to the glove, not the sofa. Rinse off the glove in the sink (with the drain catcher in place, of course).

how to wash any surface

CORK FLOORING

Fill a bucket with a few drops of dishwashing liquid or all-purpose cleanser and warm water. Then dip a cloth, a sponge, or a mop into the solution, thoroughly wring it out, and go over the cork. For tough stains, gently scrub the cork with a mop dampened with undiluted dishwashing liquid, then rinse.

CERAMIC TILE

■ For glazed tile, mix one capful of isopropyl alcohol with one gallon of water and apply the solution to the surface using a cloth or a mop. For unglazed tile, like terra-cotta, mix a few drops of dishwashing liquid into the gallon of water instead.
■ To remove stains from grout, use a nylon scrubbing pad dampened with undiluted dishwashing liquid, then rinse. For hard-to-reach stains, use an old toothbrush (electric or otherwise).

VINYL FLOORING

Clean the floor with a soft cloth or mop dipped in a solution of ½ cup of ammonia per gallon of water. Get rid of scuff marks with a sponge, nylon pad, or soft nylon brush dampened with the ammonia solution or straight isopropyl alcohol.

HARDWOOD FLOORING

■ Water and wood floors don't go hand in hand, so vacuum or sweep floors at least once a week (the longer dirt sits on the floor, the more dulling and scratching will occur).
■ When spills or scuffs appear on sealed floors, remove them with a slightly damp mop or sponge. If they're stubborn, use a bit of the cleaner the manufacturer recommends to help lift them.

5

6

7

8

how to wash any surface

BUTCHER BLOCK

Clean with a cloth or a sponge dipped in a solution of a few drops of mild detergent, such as dishwashing liquid, and warm water. Then rinse the block with plain water and pat it dry (water left on the surface can cause discoloration or warping). Bleach any stains with half of a cut lemon.

LAMINATE COUNTERTOP

Spray with an all-purpose cleanser, then wipe it down using a dampened sponge, cloth, or soft nylon pad or brush. Rinse with a clean, damp cloth. For tough stains, use an undiluted all-purpose cleanser, let it stand for a few minutes, then blot with a dampened cloth.

MARBLE

Wipe surfaces with a cloth or sponge dampened with a few drops of dishwashing liquid and warm water. Every year or so, apply a penetrating sealer (sold by stone dealers and home centers) to prevent deep stains. If any stains occur, treat with a ready-made poultice (also sold by stone dealers).

STAINLESS STEEL

Wash surfaces with a non-abrasive sponge dipped in hot water with a few drops of dishwashing liquid, working both with and against the grain to lift buildup. Dry with a towel. Next, rub on a layer of stainless-steel polish according to the package instructions, wiping off any excess immediately. Finally, with a clean, dry towel, buff the polish into the surface, going with the grain, until it shines and the towel comes away dry.

resealable plastic bag

WAX REMOVER

To freeze wax so you can remove it from a tablecloth, fill a plastic bag with ice cubes and cover the wax with it for about 20 minutes.

DOUGH SHAPER

When flattening dough for a tart or a pizza, place it in a plastic bag. Your fingers won't stick to the dough— and dough won't lodge in your nails.

SOCK STASHER

For rainy days, keep a pair of socks at work in a plastic bag. Put on the dry ones when you get to work, and carry the wet ones home in the bag.

◄ **FROSTING DISPENSER**

If you don't have a pastry bag, you can use a plastic bag to decorate a cake or cupcakes. Scoop frosting into the bag, seal it shut, snip off a tiny corner, and start piping.

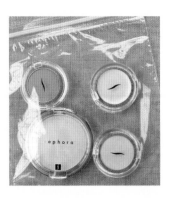

SPILL STOPPER

Prevent powder and eye shadow from getting all over your handbag by containing them (and other spill-able makeup) in a sealed plastic bag.

BUBBLE-WRAP SUBSTITUTE

Inflate a few plastic bags with a straw, seal them shut, and use them to surround semiprecious cargo before moving or shipping.

NUTCRACKER

To chop nuts en masse, dump a handful into a plastic bag, seal it shut, and run over it with a rolling pin until the nuts are of the desired size.

decorating

A dash of red lipstick or a pair of dangly earrings can liven up your look in a matter of seconds. So it should come as no surprise that a quick coat of paint, a new swatch of fabric, or a repurposed piece of furniture can do the same for your home. Here, easy ways to give any room in your house a (nearly) instant pick-me-up. No lipstick required.

114

bookshelf setup

VASES ....

Instead of banishing them to a cupboard when they're not holding flowers, keep your empty vases on the bookshelf. Cluster different sizes, shapes, and colors together to make interesting compositions. Or assemble a collection of random objects—such as a bowl, a book, and a frame—that have the same color.

BOOKS ....

■ The most useful way to arrange books is to group them first by subject (cookbooks, art books, travel books, fiction), then by subcategory (general cookbooks, cuisine-specific cookbooks), then by author.
■ Allow some room between the books and the backs of the shelves to keep air circulating and prevent the growth of mildew.
■ Forgo traditional bookends and use decorative boxes to keep books upright. Or place a stack of horizontal books flush against a row of vertical ones.

STORAGE BOXES ....

Attractive wooden or woven models—or even nice shoe boxes or gift boxes—can hold both the mundane (batteries for remote controls, matchbooks, candlesticks) and the meaningful (photos, letters, stationery).

THROWS ....

When you're not curled up with them, fold and stow throws on a bottom shelf. They give the bookcase an added dose of color and texture and look neater than when they're, well, thrown on the sofa.

PHOTOGRAPHS AND MEMORABILIA
Designate an area on your bookshelf for a
rotating art gallery of sentimental items.
Exhibit family photos, souvenirs from your
travels, funny greeting cards from friends,
or your child's latest Play-Doh creation, and
switch out the featured objects whenever
you like.

CLOCKS AND DISPLAY ITEMS
Take some of the stuff crowding your fireplace mantel or side table (such as the
clock here and the bird at left) and move it
to the bookshelf. The less typical place-
ment will render it—and the shelf—more
visually interesting and will leave the other
surfaces less cluttered.

MAGAZINES
Rather than piling back issues of your
favorite magazines on the coffee table,
stash them in a wicker basket on your
bookshelf. But limit your collection to one
medium-size basket—that way, you
won't be tempted to hold on to more
than you need.

for your living room

BETTER SEAT IN THE HOUSE

Use an old tablecloth or drape to reupholster dining-room or side chairs. Remove the seat cushion and lay it upside down on the underside of the cloth. Cut the cloth around the shape of the seat, leaving a three-inch border, then attach it securely to the bottom of the seat with a staple gun.

TRIM IN AN INSTANT

Dress up a standard monotone lamp shade by tracing a border around the top and bottom edges with a permanent marker. Apply clean-release masking tape to make sure your bands turn out straight and even.

WALL OF COLOR

Instead of covering the entire room with drop cloths and painting all four walls a new shade, try painting just one. This helps to give the room a focal point—plus, if you decide you don't love the color, it's a lot easier to change.

SOFA SPRUCE-UP ▶

To add life to a neutral sofa or hide stains on a tired one, neatly drape a colorful blanket over it and tuck it into the seat cushions (you can just let it hang freely in the back). Or place a throw over a well-worn arm.

for your bedroom

BLUE-RIBBON IDEA

Use a length of grosgrain ribbon to tie back drapes—and change colors and patterns whenever you like. You'll need a 1½-foot-long piece for each drape, and be sure to apply clear glue to the ends of the ribbons to keep them from fraying.

READY-MADE HEADBOARD

Give your bed a new backdrop with a folding screen: Just unfold it, turn it horizontally, and screw it into the wall with L-brackets. Other quick ways to make a headboard include stapling a quilt to a piece of plywood, and painting a faux version directly onto the wall.

KNOB APPEAL

Stuck with an old, boring dresser? Don't paint or replace it; resurrect it with distinctive drawer pulls made of colored glass or painted ceramic. For easy installation, choose knobs with screws that fit the existing holes.

◄ LIGHTENING UP

Mount sconces or swing-arm wall lamps on either side of the bed to reduce clutter on your bedside table (and make it nearly impossible to knock a lamp over in the dark).

for your bathroom

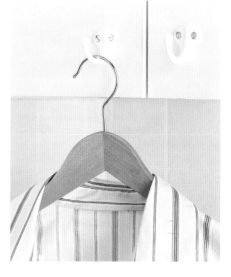

FRESH FLOWER ARRANGEMENT
To create a fast, symmetrical bouquet that will surprise and delight guests, fill a (clean) traditional toothbrush holder with water and insert an individual flower stem into each slot.

NEW TAKE ON THE TRASH CAN
Want to lend your bathroom a beachy feel? Substitute a summery enamel bucket (sold at party-supply stores) for that staid white plastic wastebasket.

HANDY HOOKS
Replace your cabinet knobs with sizable hooks, then use them to hold clothing you want to dewrinkle when you're in the shower, or hang a set of hand towels or washcloths from them.

SOAP SAVER ▶
For an elegant—and slime-free—soap dish, cover a small plate with smooth potting rocks and set the soap on top. The rocks will prevent the bar from sitting in that inevitable puddle of water.

room-by-room design diary

LIVING ROOM	KITCHEN	DINING ROOM
WALLS	WALLS	WALLS
Paint color or wallpaper style and brand:	Paint color or wallpaper style and brand:	Paint color or wallpaper style and brand:
Date painted or papered:	Date painted or papered:	Date painted or papered:
TRIM	TRIM	TRIM
Color and brand:	Color and brand:	Color and brand:
Date painted:	Date painted:	Date painted:
BLINDS, CURTAINS, OR SHADES	TILES	BLINDS, CURTAINS, OR SHADES
Color, type, and brand:	Style and brand:	Color, type, and brand:
Date installed:	Date installed:	Date installed:
WOOD FLOOR	CABINETS AND COUNTERTOPS	WOOD FLOOR
Type and stain:	Materials and brands:	Type and stain:
Last sanded and varnished:	Date installed:	Last sanded and varnished:
CARPETING OR RUG	FLOORING	CARPETING OR RUG
Style, type, and brand:	Style and brand:	Style, type, and brand:
Date installed:	Date installed:	Date installed:

For a tear-out version of this crib sheet, see the booklet on the inside back cover.

room-by-room design diary

MASTER BEDROOM	BATHROOM

PAINT PRIMER: HOW TO CHOOSE THE PERFECT WHITE

WALLS
Paint color or wallpaper style and brand:

Date painted or papered:

TRIM
Color and brand:

Date painted:

BLINDS, CURTAINS, OR SHADES
Color, type, and brand:

Date installed:

WOOD FLOOR
Type and stain:

Last sanded and varnished:

CARPETING OR RUG
Style, type, and brand:

Date installed:

WALLS
Paint color or wallpaper style and brand:

Date painted or papered:

TRIM
Color and brand:

Date painted:

TILES
Style and brand:

Date installed:

FLOORING
Style and brand:

Date installed:

FIXTURES
Styles and brands:

Date installed:

Even with the rainbow of paint colors available, white is still the ideal shade for lightening and brightening a room. But painting your walls this traditional tone isn't as simple as it seems: There are more variations of white paint on the market than of any other color. When choosing which white to use, follow these helpful selection tips:
■ Although there are exceptions, rooms that face north, and therefore away from direct sunlight, generally look better with warmer tones (undertones of yellow, cream, peach, pink, or tan). Most rooms that face south, and receive natural sunlight, should have cool tones (hints of blue, green, gray, or violet). Steer clear of stark white walls. The result can be glaring, especially if the room gets a lot of light.
■ The best way to compare whites is against a piece of pure-white paper.
■ Rather than painting a swatch directly on the wall to test the color, paint a two-by-three-foot poster board. Then move it around the room to see how it looks at different times of day and next to different pieces of furniture. (The intensity of the undertones will fluctuate with the changing light.)

wine rack

OLD USE: Cabernet and Côtes du Rhône storage.

NEW USE: Magazine holder. Roll up your current crop of periodicals and slip them into the slots. Placed alongside a sofa or a coffee table, the rack will reward you with easy-to-grab, modern-looking reading material (and the end of unsightly stacks).

binder clips

OLD USE: Paper clampers.

NEW USE: Photo, postcard, or recipe-card displayers. Simply attach two ³/₄-inch clips (or a single 1¼-inch one) to the bottom of each card for a stand-up exhibit.

sugar bowl

OLD USE: Tea and coffee companion.

NEW USE: A sweet flower vessel. Your (topless) sugar bowl is just the right size to hold a single head of hydrangea or a half-dozen sweetheart roses. Crop the stems very short so the bouquet is tight, full, and spilling over the sides.

fortune

OLD USE: Chinese-restaurant prophecy.

NEW USE: Framed inspiration. Glue a favorable fortune onto a piece of colored construction paper, then trim the paper to create a small border around the fortune (as shown above, in red). Adhere the fortune to a mat, and stick the mat in the frame.

book

OLD USE: Bedtime reading.

NEW USE: Picture-mounting assistant. To ensure that a grouping of frames is spaced evenly on a wall, use the thickness of a hardcover book as a guide.

beach towels

OLD USE: Summertime necessities.

NEW USE: Shower curtain. Instead of consigning boldly patterned beach towels to the linen closet come fall, let two of the extra-large variety (matched or not) give your bathroom a warm, sunny feel year-round. Hang the towels from a shower rod with clip-on drapery rings, and don't forget to pair them with a plastic or nylon liner.

wooden crates

OLD USE: Fruit containers.

NEW USE: Stackable storage. Convert crates that once held wine bottles or clementines into roomy nooks for toilet paper or towels.

pinecones

OLD USE: Forest-floor covering.

NEW USE: Flower-box filler. When autumn comes and the temperature dips, outdoor decorating becomes more challenging. Collect pinecones and pile them in an empty flower box for a pretty, no-maintenance display.

how to paint a room

COVER SURFACES AND WASH THE WALLS

Place a canvas drop cloth (sold at hardware stores) on the floor, and drape plastic drop cloths over any furniture. Then, since dust, dirt, and grease spots can ruin a smooth finish, clean your walls with a cellulose sponge dipped in water and a little mild dishwashing detergent. Rinse with clean water to remove any soap residue.

TAPE ALONG EDGES

Use blue painter's tape, which doesn't leave any residue and can be applied up to a week ahead of time, to protect the trim, the ceiling, and the frames of windows and doors.

PRIME THE WALLS

Unfortunately, it's just a myth that walls don't need to be primed if they have been painted many times. In fact, primer helps maximize the sheen and coverage of paint and gives the finish a more uniform look. So apply a coat before painting.

BRUSH WHERE YOU CAN'T ROLL

Before starting on the centers of the walls, first paint the corners and next to anywhere there is painter's tape with a two-inch angled brush. Paint a two-to-three-inch border around windows, corners, doors, trim, and the ceiling.

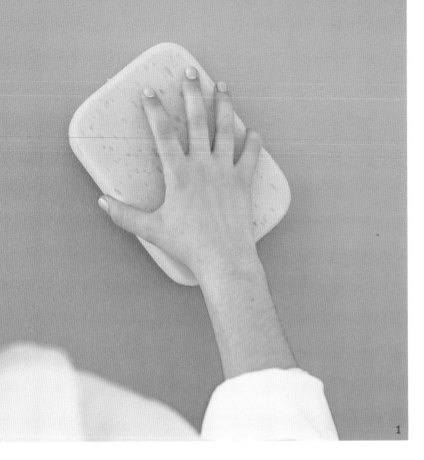

1

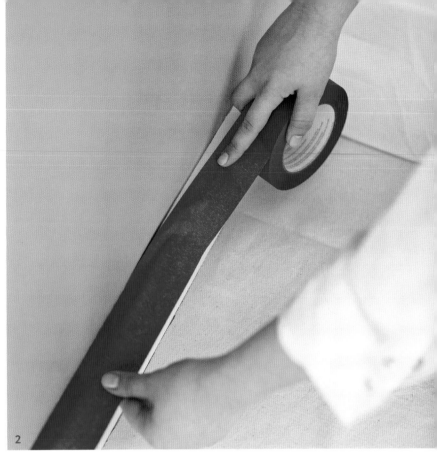

2

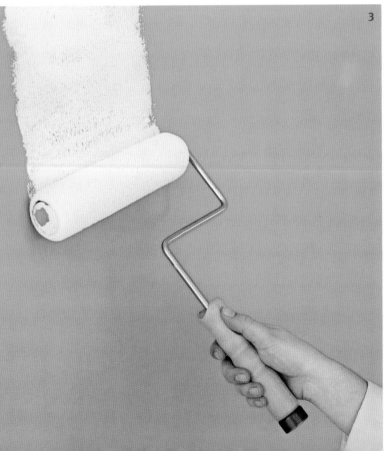

3

4

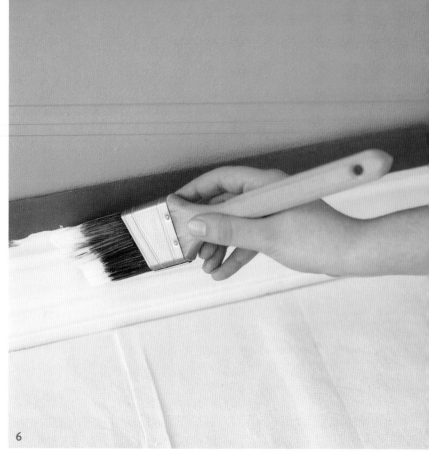

SUNSET

how to paint a room

USE THE W TECHNIQUE

Now you're ready to start on the centers of the walls with a roller. For a quick and even application, begin at one side of a wall and roll on a three-by-three-foot W pattern, then fill it in without lifting the roller. Continue in sections. Immediately after you've finished painting, remove the painter's tape slowly and carefully, so you don't peel away any paint with it.

PAINT THE TRIM

Wait until the walls are completely dry, then apply new strips of painter's tape to where the trim meets the wall (the tape will now be on the newly painted wall). Use a two-inch angled brush to paint moldings, door frames, and window frames. If you're also painting the baseboards, place strips of tape along the floor as well as on the newly painted wall.

CLEAN THE PAINT-CAN RIM

With a screwdriver wrapped in a rag, clean off the rim of the paint can. (If there is paint left in the rim's groove, you won't be able to seal the lid tightly, and any leftover paint will dry out.)

SEAL AND LABEL THE CAN

Cover the open can with plastic wrap to create a tight seal, put the lid in place, then pound it with a hammer. Dab a little paint on the lid with your rag or a paintbrush to remind you of the color. Then write the paint's name or number on the lid with a permanent marker so you can reorder it if necessary.

lemon

TABLE ENHANCER
A dozen lemons mixed with a pound of hazelnuts in a glass bowl makes a glowing table topper. Add a few branches of lemon leaves, if desired.

CUTTING-BOARD BLEACHER
Rub half a cut lemon over a wooden or plastic cutting board to clean and whiten the surface. Then rinse.

BROWNING PREVENTER
Sprinkle apple or pear slices with lemon juice after cutting, or squeeze some lemon juice into just-made guacamole and stir.

◄ **GRATER CLEANER**
After shredding soft cheese or other sticky foods, go over both sides of the grater with the pulp side of a cut lemon to get rid of any residue.

HAIR LIGHTENER
For a subtle highlighter for blond hair, simmer two sliced lemons in water for one hour (add more water if needed). Strain, then pour into a spray bottle.

SORE-THROAT SOOTHER
Roast a halved lemon over a flame until the peel turns golden. Remove from the heat, then mix the juice with one teaspoon of honey. Drink.

LAUNDRY BRIGHTENER
Skip the bleach—add $1/4$ to $1/2$ cup of lemon juice to the wash cycle to lighten whites.

entertaining

It's only fitting that people *throw* parties. Throwing implies physical effort, and parties, as any good hostess worth her crudités knows, can be exhausting. But you don't have to go through the evening running on empty (in high heels, no less). These party tricks take the pain out of entertaining—and leave you with plenty of energy for the conga line.

party-throwing necessities

GLASSWARE

Stow these five styles (shown from left to right) in a cupboard to cover all types of beverages. To minimize the time you spend over a suds-filled sink, opt for dishwasher-safe versions when possible.

■ Wineglasses for white and red wine (basic 10-ounce glasses will work for both)
■ Old-fashioned or lowball glasses for juice and drinks on the rocks
■ Tumblers or highball glasses for sparkling water, cola, Bloody Marys, and vodka or gin and tonics
■ Pint glasses for beer, cider, lemonade, and iced coffee
■ Champagne flutes for Champagne, mimosas, and Bellinis

LIST OF TASKS TO DELEGATE

Instead of drawing a blank, refer to this list when hovering guests ask, "What can I do?" (Tape it to the inside of your cupboard or a cabinet for easy reference.) Chores to pawn off: lighting candles, opening wine, taking arriving guests' coats, refilling the ice bucket, arranging the cheese platter, and tossing the salad.

TRIVETS

Stash different sizes for different dishes, including at least a couple that you can push together for large hot casseroles.

SERVING PIECES

Stock basic plates, platters, and bowls to complement whatever you're serving.
■ Cake stands for cheese and crackers before dinner and for desserts after
■ Assorted platters and trays for sliced meats, vegetables, cookies, and fruit
■ Small dishes, cups, or ramekins for dips, nuts, candies, and olives (remember to provide an extra one for the pits)

1. LIGHT CANDLES
2. OPEN WINE
3. TAKE COATS
4. ARRANGE CHEESE PLATTER
5. TOSS SALAD

CHINESE-TAKEOUT CONTAINERS

Send guests home with leftovers rather than trying to cram everything into your fridge. Use either the typical white paper ones or the sturdier translucent plastic versions (both are sold at party-supply stores).

CANDLES

Have a healthy supply of tapers and birthday candles at the ready, along with unscented pillars in different sizes. And don't forget matches.

CORKSCREW AND BOTTLE OPENER

Move these indispensable tools out of that cluttered kitchen drawer and near your party supplies for easy access.

SERVING UTENSILS

Store a selection of cheese and dip spreaders, forks, and spoons with the trays and platters.

STAIN-FIGHTING KIT

To combat inevitable spills, keep the following in a box or a plastic container: a sponge, talcum powder, isopropyl alcohol, Shout spray, a small bottle filled with one part white vinegar and one part water, and a clean cloth or white paper towels. (For tips on stain removal, see page 100.)

PAPER COCKTAIL NAPKINS

For ease and versatility, choose any-season, any-occasion colors (such as white, cream, or blue), and buy them in bulk.

TABLE LINENS

Group cloth napkins by count (6, 8, 12) and tablecloths by shape (oblong, oval, square). That way, you won't have to upturn the entire stack when looking for the set that matches your needs.

for centerpieces

BOX SET

To make a wither-resistant display, tie up stacks of small white gift boxes (sold at party-supply stores) with colorful, seasonal ribbons. Feeling especially generous? Slip chocolates inside each box and give the boxes to guests as party favors.

A FLATTERING LIGHT

Cluster unscented pillar candles of various heights and diameters on a tray or platter, or even atop a mirror or a simple terra-cotta plant saucer.

GARDEN PARTY

To create a fresh, fragrant setting, place potted herbs (such as rosemary, shown above) down the center of the table. Also good to try: thyme, mint, or a flowering annual, such as white geraniums.

AUTUMN HARVEST ▶

Arrange stems of dried magnolia leaves (sold at garden centers) in a galvanized bucket for a casual, organic feel. Include stems of different lengths to provide shape and volume.

[JANE]

for place settings

EASY AS ABC

For a casual dinner with friends, children's magnetic letters are a playful way to indicate each guest's spot. Use the first letter of the person's name—or of the first and last names if you happened to invite Jamie, Joy, and Jennifer.

GOOD ENOUGH TO EAT

Welcome friends and family to the table with red, purple, or green pears (or some other seasonal fruit). Just tie the name tags to the stems with ribbon.

TAG ALONG

This luggage identifier makes for both a surprising place marker and a practical party favor. Label each tag, pull the napkin through the strap, and center the bundle on a plate.

◀ TABLE LABEL

Want a split-second suggestion? Write names directly onto a paper tablecloth. Bonus: If you set the table with paper plates and cups and plastic utensils, you can wrap up the whole spread afterward and throw it in the garbage bin.

145

for drinks

LIP SERVICE

An easy way to jazz up old standby beverages is to add unexpected flavors to the rims of the glasses. Dip margarita glasses in sea salt and lime zest (as shown above), coat the edge of a Champagne flute in sugar, or sprinkle celery salt and cayenne along the rim of a Bloody Mary.

SWEET STIRRERS

For a fun twist on cocktail accessories, stock up on lollipops in colors and flavors that will match your drinks (for example, cherry pops for cranberry juice and vodka). Unwrap the pops and stick them in the glasses, candy-side down.

A TREAT FOR THE TEETOTALER

Serve pear, apricot, or passion-fruit spritzers to nondrinkers and designated drivers. Simply mix a shot of fruit nectar (sold at gourmet grocery stores) with nonalcoholic sparkling wine or sparkling water and top with ice.

CHILLING EFFECTS ▶

Freeze berries in an ice-cube tray to use in place of ice. They look stunning in fizzy beverages, won't water down drinks, and provide a burst of flavor— not to mention a dose of antioxidants.

cocktail-party quantities

	ITEM	PARTY FOR 6	PARTY FOR 12	PARTY FOR 24	WHAT ELSE TO HAVE ON HAND
ALCOHOL	Beer	2 six-packs	3 six-packs	4 six-packs	■ Bottle opener
	White wine	2 750-milliliter bottles	4 750-milliliter bottles	8 750-milliliter bottles	■ Corkscrew
	Red wine	2 750-milliliter bottles	4 750-milliliter bottles	8 750-milliliter bottles	■ Cocktail spoon (or swizzle sticks)
	Bourbon	1 750-milliliter bottle	1 750-milliliter bottle	2 750-milliliter bottles	■ Standard cocktail shaker
	Gin	1 750-milliliter bottle	2 750-milliliter bottles	3 750-milliliter bottles	■ Jigger (or shot glass)
	Rum	1 750-milliliter bottle	2 750-milliliter bottles	3 750-milliliter bottles	■ Peeler (for twists)
	Scotch (blended)	1 750-milliliter bottle	1 750-milliliter bottle	2 750-milliliter bottles	■ Juicer
	Vermouth (dry)	1 750-milliliter bottle	1 750-milliliter bottle	1 750-milliliter bottle	■ Cutting board
	Vodka	1 750-milliliter bottle	2 750-milliliter bottles	3 750-milliliter bottles	■ Paring knife
	Whiskey	1 750-milliliter bottle	1 750-milliliter bottle	1 750-milliliter bottle	■ Cocktail napkins
MIXERS	Club soda or seltzer	2 1-liter bottles	3 1-liter bottles	6 1-liter bottles	
	Cola and diet cola	1 1-liter bottle each	2 1-liter bottles each	3 1-liter bottles each	
	Cranberry juice	1 quart	2 quarts	3 quarts	
	Ginger ale	1 1-liter bottle	1 1-liter bottle	2 1-liter bottles	
	Orange juice	1 quart	2 quarts	3 quarts	
	Tonic water	2 1-liter bottles	3 1-liter bottles	6 1-liter bottles	
ICE, GARNISHES, AND GLASSES	Ice	6 pounds	12 pounds	24 pounds	
	Lemons and limes	2 each	3 each	4 each	
	Olives	1 6.75-ounce jar	1 6.75-ounce jar	2 6.75-ounce jars	
	Wineglasses	6	12	24	
	Tumblers	6	12	24	

For a tear-out version of this crib sheet, see the booklet on the inside back cover.

easy hors d'oeuvre ideas

PARTY FOR 6	PARTY FOR 12	PARTY FOR 24
8 ounces soft cheese	2 8-ounce pieces soft cheese	2 16-ounce pieces soft cheese
8 ounces semihard cheese	2 8-ounce pieces semihard cheese	2 16-ounce pieces semihard cheese
8 ounces hard cheese	2 8-ounce pieces hard cheese	2 16-ounce pieces hard cheese
1 box assorted crackers	2 boxes assorted crackers	4 boxes assorted crackers
3 sliced pears or apples	4 sliced pears or apples	8 sliced pears or apples
1 small bowl of nuts or dried fruits	2 small bowls of nuts and/or dried fruits	4 small bowls of nuts and/or dried fruits
1/2 loaf crusty bread	1 loaf crusty bread	2 loaves crusty bread

CHEESE-SERVING TIPS

■ Take the cheeses out of the refrigerator one to two hours before you serve them, since the cold mutes flavors.

■ Provide a spreading knife for cutting soft cheeses (like chèvre or Brie), a paring knife for semihard cheeses (like blue cheese or Cheddar), and a cheese shaver for hard cheeses (like Asiago or Parmesan).

■ Refrigerate leftovers right away. Store soft cheeses in plastic containers (to retain moisture). Wrap semihard cheeses in waxed paper (so they're able to breathe) and hard cheeses in plastic wrap (so they don't dry out).

MINI PIZZAS
START WITH: A large cheese pizza (ask for it unsliced and, if it's possible, slightly underbaked).
TO MAKE: Avoiding the crust, stamp out small rounds of pizza with a circular cookie or biscuit cutter. Heat the rounds at 400° F for about five minutes. Then top with olive slices, chopped prosciutto, marinated mushrooms, an anchovy fillet, or fresh herbs (such as basil, rosemary, flat-leaf parsley, or oregano).

MEDITERRANEAN BRUSCHETTA
START WITH: Garlic bread from an Italian restaurant (or frozen garlic bread, thawed).
TO MAKE: Toast in a 350° F oven or toaster oven for about five minutes, or until golden. Top it with prepared pesto, goat cheese, mozzarella, marinated peppers, or oil-packed sun-dried tomatoes.

GUACAMOLE-STUFFED CHERRY TOMATOES
START WITH: Fresh guacamole from a gourmet market.
TO MAKE: Take a pint of cherry tomatoes, cut off the tops, and scoop out the seeds. Then slice a thin disk off the bottom of each tomato to help it stand up. Fill each with a dollop of guacamole, and top with a small cilantro leaf.

CHICKEN OR SHRIMP BOATS
START WITH: A chicken or shrimp stir-fry from a Chinese restaurant.
TO MAKE: Mound spoonfuls of stir-fry into the cuplike center leaves from a head of Boston lettuce. Top the boats with nuts or sliced scallions.

SESAME SPARERIBS
START WITH: A couple of orders of Chinese spareribs.
TO MAKE: Separate the spareribs and roll them in sesame seeds. Then heat them on a lined baking sheet in a 300° F oven for about 10 minutes, or until warm.

ceramic mugs

OLD USE: Coffee accessories.

NEW USE: Utensil containers. Recruit sturdy mugs to store spoons, forks, and knives on a buffet table or to transport them to the dining room for table setting (this is especially helpful for outdoor dining or if setting the table is a child's chore).

spaghetti

OLD USE: Wednesday-night dinner.

NEW USE: Candle lighter. If you're short on matches, a strand of raw spaghetti is a surefire—and longer-lasting—substitute (just be patient; it can take a few seconds to ignite). Spaghetti is also ideal for the fireplace, since its length allows you to safely light the hard-to-reach spots.

washing machine

OLD USE: Clothes cleaner.

NEW USE: Beverage cooler. If there's no room in the refrigerator for drinks, fill your washing machine with water, add ice, and load in bottles and cans. When the party's over, allow the ice to melt, then run the spin cycle to drain the water.

cloth napkins

OLD USE: Lap shielders.

NEW USE: Drink coasters. When cloth napkins become overly stained, cut them into $5^{1}/_{2}$-inch squares with pinking shears and let them protect your tables at parties. To make a longer-lasting version, lay a napkin flat on a piece of felt and use the shears to cut the square out of both pieces of fabric. Apply fabric glue to the edges and across the middle of the felt piece, then press the napkin to the felt.

baby spoons

OLD USE: Toddler utensils.

NEW USE: Condiment servers. For burger fixings, salad dressings, or party dips, these small spoons are utilitarian but sophisticated alternatives to messy jars and squeeze bottles.

ketchup bottle

OLD USE: Diner icon.

NEW USE: Plate decorator. Fill a clean plastic ketchup or mustard bottle (sold at kitchen-supply stores) with raspberry, chocolate, or caramel sauce and use it to embellish a dessert plate (or the confection itself) with zigzags, swirls, or polka dots.

cake stands

OLD USE: Occasional pedestals for baked goods.
NEW USE: Party-food holders. Stack a small cake stand on top of a larger one, then stock the tiers with finger sandwiches, canapés, or crudités.

skinny pretzels

OLD USE: Beer buddies.
NEW USE: Edible toothpicks. Use pretzel sticks in place of wooden skewers to spear bite-size meatballs or mozzarella balls and cherry tomatoes. The best part: You won't have to fish discarded toothpicks out of your planters after the party.

how to set a table

1

START WITH THE PLATES

Position the dinner plate squarely in the middle of the place setting (directly in front of the chair). Place the bread plate and the butter knife above and to the left of the dinner plate (with the butter knife resting on the bread plate). Fold the napkin and lay it to the left of the dinner plate, with the folded edge facing away from the plate.

2

POSITION THE DINNER UTENSILS

Set the smaller salad fork and the larger dinner fork to the left of the dinner plate, resting them on top of the napkin (if the napkin is in a napkin ring, the forks should go between the napkin and the plate). Place the dinner knife and the soupspoon to the right of the plate (with the knife's blade facing the plate). Always arrange the utensils in the order they'll be used, from the outside in.

3

ADD THE GLASSES

Set the wineglass and the water glass above and to the right of the dinner plate. The wineglass should be the closest glass to the plate, with the water glass above and slightly to the left of it. Hint: If all these guidelines escape you when you're minutes away from a dinner party, just remember "BMW," which stands for "bread, meal, and water," in that order from left to right.

4

FINISH WITH THE DESSERT UTENSILS

It's perfectly acceptable to bring dessert spoons and forks to the table when dessert is being served, but if you'd like to have them on the table for the duration of the meal, place them above the plate, with the spoon on top and pointing to the left, and the fork below with its prongs pointing to the right.

1

2

3

4

coffee filter

SNACK SERVER

Fill a bunch of coffee filters with popcorn, pretzels, or other finger food, and set them on a tray or a table for a kids' party.

SOIL SAVER

Keep soil from draining out of a flowerpot by inserting a coffee filter in the bottom, over the drainage hole, when repotting the plant.

CORK CATCHER

If broken cork is floating in your wine bottle, position a cone-shaped coffee filter over a pitcher or a carafe and slowly strain the wine through it.

◄ **PLATE PROTECTOR**

To prevent chipping and scratching, place a flattened coffee filter between fragile or hand-painted dishes, as well as pieces of nonstick cookware.

DIP MAKER

Secure a filter over a glass and use it to strain plain yogurt. Then mix the thickened yogurt with chopped garlic, parsley, salt, and pepper.

PREP HELPER

Coffee filters can hold dry goods like raw vegetables, herbs, or chocolate when you're cooking or baking. That way, you'll have fewer bowls to wash.

SCREEN CLEANER

For lint-free viewing, grab a coffee filter to regularly wipe down dusty and staticky computer monitors and TV screens.

celebrating

Why is it that planning a special occasion takes weeks, even months, when the event itself lasts a nanosecond? You spend so much time preparing that you miss the big picture (Wait, *whose* birthday is it?) and, quite frankly, a lot of the fun. Not anymore. With some deft shortcuts and fresh takes on traditions, you can have your cake and eat it, too.

gift-wrapping kit

WRAPPING PAPER ....
Rather than buying (and storing) countless rolls of paper covered in Santas or storks, use general white kraft paper to wrap year-round. Rely on ribbons and tags to tie the presents to a particular event or holiday.

DOUBLE-SIDED TAPE ....
Wrapping professionals swear by this invisible secret weapon. It gives any gift a seamless, finished look.

SCISSORS ....
Squirrel away a pair of sharp scissors specifically for wrapping (and *not* for gluey school projects).

HOLE PUNCH ....
This standard-issue office tool can punch holes in homemade gift tags—or along the tops of gift bags, so you can insert ribbons and tie bows.

BROWN PAPER BAGS

These lunchtime mainstays are perfect for "wrapping" fragile or odd-shaped gifts (such as ornaments, cookies, or stuffed animals) in an instant. Adorn them with pretty tags and bows. (For easy bag-decorating ideas, see page 164.)

GIFT TAGS

Keeping a few store-bought tags on hand is a good idea, but you can also make your own from Valentine's Day, Christmas, or thank-you cards you have received (like the cards shown at top left). Cut out whatever design is on the front, then write your message on the back, punch a hole in the corner, and string a ribbon through.

RIBBONS

Stock them in assorted colors, sizes, and textures, from raffia to thin curling ribbon to wider fabric styles. Though slightly pricey, grosgrain, with its ridged surface, is especially easy to tie—and it can be reused.

for christmas

STRING THEORY

You'll get fuller, more even coverage— and make post-holiday light removal a lot easier—if you string your Christmas-tree lights from the bottom of the tree to the top and back down again (rather than in a circle) and weave the strings in and out of the branches from trunk to tip.

BRING HOME THE DOUGH

Give your rolling pin a rest and opt for store-bought slice-and-bake Christmas cookies. Dress them up with almonds and raw sugar (as shown above) or mini M&Ms in the shape of a tree, or dip them in melted white chocolate and sprinkle on silver balls.

THEY'RE IN THE BAG

When a gift's shape defies wrapping, (or your timetable prevents it), turn everyday paper sacks into charming parcels. Punch holes or cut slits into the tops of the bags and thread in some decorative ribbon, then attach cheerful gift tags.

MINTY ADDITIONS ▶

To lend some festive flavor to a cold-weather treat, repurpose standard-size candy canes as hot-chocolate stirrers.

for other holidays and birthdays

PARTY FAVORS ON DISPLAY

Fill a glass bowl with seasonal treats to use as a centerpiece, then let guests take the goodies home with them. Go with blowers and breath mints for New Year's Eve (and the midnight kiss), or small gourds and candy corn for Halloween.

◄ **PERSONALIZED PAPER**

To give your gifts signature style, wrap them in maps, comics, or wedding announcements (spritz hair spray on the newspaper to lock in the ink). Or enlarge dictionary entries on a copier (try *love* for an anniversary, or *hero* for Father's Day).

CAKE AND ICE CREAM IN ONE

Instead of mixing up the typical—and time-consuming—buttercream, frost birthday cupcakes with ice cream. Let your chosen flavor soften for a few minutes, then cream it by hand with a rubber spatula until it has the consistency of frosting. Spread it onto the cupcakes, and place them in the freezer for one hour to harden before serving.

HEARTFELT MESSAGES

Enlist everyday items to create clever cards. For example, make valentines out of Red Hots boxes (*I have the hots for you*), heart-shaped soaps (*I'm awash in your love*), or even matchbooks (*Light my fire*).

important friend-and-family dates

Use this worksheet to record birthdays, anniversaries, and other notable dates. Keep it in a visible spot and it will serve as a helpful (not to mention face-saving) reminder for years to come.

JANUARY		FEBRUARY		MARCH	
Name	Date	Name	Date	Name	Date
Name	Date	Name	Date	Name	Date
Name	Date	Name	Date	Name	Date
Name	Date	Name	Date	Name	Date

APRIL		MAY		JUNE	
Name	Date	Name	Date	Name	Date
Name	Date	Name	Date	Name	Date
Name	Date	Name	Date	Name	Date
Name	Date	Name	Date	Name	Date

JULY		AUGUST		SEPTEMBER	
Name	Date	Name	Date	Name	Date
Name	Date	Name	Date	Name	Date
Name	Date	Name	Date	Name	Date
Name	Date	Name	Date	Name	Date

OCTOBER		NOVEMBER		DECEMBER	
Name	Date	Name	Date	Name	Date
Name	Date	Name	Date	Name	Date
Name	Date	Name	Date	Name	Date
Name	Date	Name	Date	Name	Date

For a tear-out version of this crib sheet, see the booklet on the inside back cover.

helpful holiday hints

VALENTINE'S DAY	MOTHER'S DAY/FATHER'S DAY	MEMORIAL DAY
■ Order online flower arrangements a week ahead of time so you won't incur rush-shipping charges. ■ Remember to have a shoe box on hand for your child's classroom valentines. ■ If you want to savor your chocolates beyond a week or two, roll them tightly in plastic wrap, place them in an airtight container, and freeze.	■ Write the honoree's card the weekend before, so you have time to say what you really mean. ■ For a more enduring option (and because you already sent flowers on Valentine's Day), give your mother a young flowering shrub or tree. Ones that blossom in the spring include crab-apple, cherry, and redbud trees and azalea bushes. ■ Sign your father up for a gift-of-the-month club, such as fruit, cheese, coffee, beer, or wine.	■ Clean your American flag. Soak a nylon or poly-ester flag in warm water and Woolite, then machine wash it (if yours is made of cotton or linen, it doesn't need to be presoaked). Air-dry. ■ Hose down or dust outdoor furniture to prepare for backyard lounging and alfresco dining. ■ Stock up on a season's worth of charcoal (or fill your gas tank to the brim) for summer grilling.
FOURTH OF JULY	LABOR DAY	HALLOWEEN
■ Buy cherries in June, when they are at their peak. Pit and freeze them for your all-American cherry pie on Independence Day. ■ If you're having a picnic, make an oil-based pasta salad, not a mayonnaise-based potato salad, to avoid quick spoilage. ■ Get to the fireworks display early to claim a good spot. Don't forget blankets, chairs, and bug spray.	■ Clip a grill light onto your grill to make outdoor cooking easier as the days get shorter (sigh). ■ Instead of the typical butter-and-salt combina-tion, try topping ears of corn with ground cayenne and lime juice, or olive oil and grated Parmesan. ■ Take advantage of the end-of-summer sales and buy flip-flops and beach towels, totes, and chairs for next year.	■ Carve your pumpkin no more than three days be-fore Halloween so it won't be rotten by the big night. ■ Be sure you have extra flashlight batteries and reflective tape at the ready for trick-or-treating. ■ Snap a photograph of the whole family decked out in Halloween costumes, and use it for this year's holiday card. You can skip that last-minute photo-op in December, and your season's greetings will be fresher and funnier.
THANKSGIVING	CHRISTMAS	NEW YEAR'S EVE
■ When making gravy, place the turkey drippings in the freezer for about 10 minutes to speed up the separation of the fat from the broth. ■ Store cleaning supplies in every bathroom, for quick wipe-downs before guests arrive. ■ Take table linens to the dry cleaner at least a week before the feast, and set aside time the weekend before to polish the silver.	■ Buy small gifts in bulk. Choose a favorite bottle of olive oil or balsamic vinegar to give to all those party hostesses, neighbors, and unexpected visitors. ■ Get your seasonal stamps online to avoid waiting at the post office, and mail your holiday cards by December 18. ■ For a more relaxed holiday party, invite guests for Sunday afternoon. (Saturday nights often book up fast in December, anyway.)	■ Make a playlist or a mix tape for your party. With guests to greet and Champagne corks to pop, you won't have time to DJ. ■ To chill Champagne quickly, place it in a bucket of ice water rather than just straight ice. ■ If you're attending someone else's New Year's party, bring the host a morning-after basket of teas and coffee, muffins or scones, and a bottle of aspirin. And send a handwritten thank-you note.

jump rope

OLD USE: Double-Dutch device.

NEW USE: Ribbon. Tie a jump rope around a child's present for a fun and sporty finishing touch. Want a sweeter idea? Try a pair of candy necklaces.

candy canes

OLD USE: Stocking stuffers.

NEW USE: Valentine's Day cupcake toppers. Form hearts out of mini candy canes and bake for two to four minutes at 350° F on a nonstick baking sheet. Once the canes are warm to the touch, pinch the ends together, then let the hearts cool and place them atop your cupcakes.

life savers

OLD USE: Sugar-craving fix.

NEW USE: Candle holders. To protect your cake from wax drippings, stick the bottoms of birthday candles into Life Savers and set the stable bases on the cake. (Be sure to get the Life Savers that are sold in rolls—the individually wrapped ones that come in bags are too big.)

straw

OLD USE: Sipping cola.

NEW USE: Hole punch. If you'd like your Christmas cookies to double as edible tree ornaments, use a straw to poke holes in them before baking. Afterward, run a ribbon through each hole to hang them.

clothespins

OLD USE: Wet-laundry clips.

NEW USE: Holiday-card displayers. Adhere a wide gros-grain ribbon to the wall with double-sided mounting tape, then attach holiday cards up and down it for a jolly—and changeable—seasonal exhibit. Both regular-size and mini clothespins (shown here) will work.

paper shredder

OLD USE: Document destroyer.

NEW USE: Confetti maker. Feed colorful gift-wrapping tissue through your shredder to produce instant Easter-basket grass or padding for a present.

paper-towel stand

OLD USE: Handy sheet dispenser.

NEW USE: Ribbon organizer. For easy access when you're wrapping, slide spools of ribbon with at least a one-inch-diameter opening onto the towel stand's post. Stack the spools from large to small, bottom to top, and tape the ribbon ends to their spools when you're not using them.

foil cupcake holders

OLD USE: Batter containers.

NEW USE: Snack distributors. Fill sturdy foil cupcake holders with mixed nuts, mints, hard candy, or candy corn, and scatter them around a party. Or, to make kids swoon at a birthday, place an individual cupcake holder at each setting.

how to carve a bird

1

REMOVE THE LEG
Place the turkey or chicken on a cutting board that has a trough to catch the juices. With a carving knife, cut through the crispy skin that connects the leg and the breast and slice down, using the knife to pull the leg away from the body (a carving fork can help stabilize the bird). Continue until you reach the joint, and cut through it to separate the leg. Set the leg aside.

2

REMOVE THE BREAST MEAT
Ideally, you'll want to get this side of breast meat off in one piece. Slowly and steadily slide the knife along one side of the breastbone, as close to the bone as possible. Then cut the breast off of the rest of the body.

3

SLICE THE BREAST MEAT
Remove the rest of the bird from the cutting board and set it aside. Place the breast meat on the board and slice it thinly, then transfer the meat to a platter.

4

SEPARATE THE THIGH, DRUMSTICK, AND WING
Place the leg back on the board. Cut through the joint between the thigh and the drumstick, then slice the meat from the thigh and transfer it and the drumstick to the platter. Place the bird back on the cutting board and detach the wing where it connects to the body; transfer it to the platter. Repeat steps 1 to 4 on the other side of the bird.

dental floss

SOFT-CHEESE CUTTER
Instead of constantly having to wipe off your knife, try unflavored waxed floss to slice disks of soft cheese or to divide a cheesecake into neat wedges.

VINE WINDER
Because it's resilient, dental floss is ideal for training vines on a trellis. Be careful not to tie the floss too tightly or it will dig into the growing stem.

PHOTO SAVER
To separate old photos from those "magnetic" album pages without tearing the pictures, slide waxed floss between the photo and the page.

◄ **CAKE SLICER**
When a recipe calls for splitting a cake in two horizontally, use a two-foot piece of unflavored waxed dental floss to make a clean, straight cut.

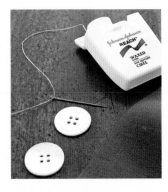

THREAD SUBSTITUTE
Rely on waxed dental floss for temporary but durable clothing repairs, such as replacing missing buttons or reattaching a strap.

CHICKEN BINDER
When you're out of kitchen twine (or if you never had any in the first place), unflavored unwaxed floss is a perfect stand-in for trussing a bird.

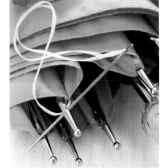

UMBRELLA MENDER
If your umbrella has detached from its metal spines, tie or sew it back together with waxed floss, which will endure longer than regular thread.

BEACH POINT
DAY CAMP
2002
SHELL HUNT

JACK'S
FOSSILS

2003

JACK'S
SEASHELLS

SUMMER 2004

BEACH POINT
DAY CAMP
2002
SHELL HUNT

MORE
JACK'S
TREASURES

JACK'S
TREASURES

JACK'S
NECKLACE +
MEDALLIONS
2003

MARBLES
WARREN, VT
AUGUST 2004

JACK'S
TREASURES
SUMMER 2004

photography credits

ANTONIS ACHILLEOS page 7; pages 10 to 11; page 12, left; page 12, middle; page 13; page 15, right; page 20, right; page 21, left; page 22, left; page 23, left; page 23, right; page 26; page 27, top left; page 27, top middle; page 27, bottom left; page 27, bottom middle; page 27, bottom right; pages 30 to 31; page 32, right; page 33; page 34; page 35, left; page 40, right; page 41, left; page 41, right; page 42, left; page 42, right; page 47, top left; page 47, bottom left; page 47, bottom middle; page 49; pages 50 to 51; page 52, right; page 53; page 54; page 55, middle; page 55, right; page 56, right; page 57; page 59; page 60; page 62, left; page 62, right; page 63, left; page 63, right; page 64, right; page 70; page 71, top middle; page 71, top right; page 71, bottom left; page 71, bottom middle; page 73; page 76, left; page 76, middle; page 76, right; page 77; page 78; page 79, left; page 79, middle; page 79, right; page 82; page 85, left; page 86, left; page 86, right; page 89, top left; page 89, bottom right; page 91, top middle; page 91, top right; page 91, bottom right; pages 94 to 95; page 96, left; page 97; page 98; page 99, middle; page 99, right; page 101; page 102; page 105, left; page 105, right; page 107, left; page 107, right; page 109, top left; page 110, top left; page 110, top right; page 110, bottom left; page 112; page 113, top right; page 115; pages 116 to 117; page 118, right; page 119; page 121, left; page 121, right; page 122, middle; page 123; page 129, left; page 130, left; page 130, right; page 131, left; page 137, bottom right; page 139; pages 140 to 141; page 142, left; page 142, right; page 144; page 145, middle; page 146, left; page 146, middle; page 146, right; page 147; page 152, left; page 153, right; page 154, right; page 155, left; page 155,

right; page 157; page 158; page 159, bottom middle; page 159, bottom right; page 161; pages 162 to 163; page 167, left; page 167, right; page 169; page 170; page 174, right; page 175, left; page 175, right; page 178; page 179, top middle; page 179, top right; page 179, bottom middle; page 179, bottom right

SANG AN page 56, left; page 56, middle

JAMES BAIGRIE page 21, right; page 46; page 47, top middle; page 47, bottom right; page 65, left; page 89, top right; page 90; page 91, top left; page 91, bottom middle; page 104, left; page 113, top left; page 113, top middle; page 113, bottom left; page 131, right; page 136; page 137, top right; page 159, top left; page 173, left; page 177

MARY ELLEN BARTLEY page 173, right

ANDREW BORDWIN page 190

MONICA BUCK page 4; page 37; page 43, right; page 93; page 125; page 179, bottom left

ANITA CALERO page 71, bottom right; page 84, left; page 149

JENNIFER CAUSEY page 89, bottom left

DASHA EWING page 67; page 68

MARILI FORASTIERI page 25

FORMULA Z/S page 15, middle; page 22, right; page 35, right; page 52, left; page 52, middle; page 145, left; page 154, left; page 164, middle

BETH GALTON page 12, right; page 20, left

THAYER ALLYSON GOWDY page 113, bottom right; page 159, top middle

PERRY HAGOPIAN page 18

AIMEE HERRING page 17

BOB HIEMSTRA page 29

FRANCES JANISCH page 32, middle; page 85, right; page 104, right; page 118, middle; page 128, left

PETER LAMASTRO page 45; page 91, bottom left

RICK LEW page 113, bottom middle; page 137, top middle; page 159, bottom left; page 166; page 179, top left

MARK LUND page 87, left; page 128, right

MICHAEL LUPPINO page 129, right

CHARLES MARAIA page 137, bottom middle

ANDREW McCAUL page 65, right; page 109, top right; page 109, bottom right; page 122, left; page 153, left

MAURA McEVOY page 137, top left; page 142, middle; page 143; page 165

FERNANDO MILANI page 38

AMY NEUNSINGER page 14

ANNA PALMA page 15, left; page 35, middle

BILL PHELPS page 32, left

DAVID PRINCE page 64, left; page 71, top left; page 87, right; page 118, left; page 122, right; page 180

ALEXANDRA ROWLEY page 40, left; page 43, left; page 55, left; page 81; page 109, bottom left; page 110, bottom right; page 152, right; page 172, left

FRANCE RUFFENACH page 106, left; page 137, bottom left

ANNIE SCHLECHTER page 184; page 189

ELLEN SILVERMAN pages 74 to 75; page 126; page 145, right; page 164, left; page 164, right; page 174, left

ANN STRATTON page 106, right

MIKKEL VANG page 96, middle; page 96, right; page 99, left

WILLIAM WALDRON page 9

WENDELL T. WEBBER page 133; page 134

MARK WEISS page 27, top right; page 47, top right; page 84, right; page 159, top right; page 172, right

PAUL WHICHELOE page 120; page 121, middle

ANNA WILLIAMS page 150; page 167, middle

REAL SIMPLE
MANAGING EDITOR Kristin van Ogtrop
CREATIVE DIRECTOR Vanessa Holden
SPECIAL PROJECTS EDITOR Sarah Humphreys
ART DIRECTOR Ivette Montes de Oca
COPY EDITOR Myles McDonnell
RESEARCH EDITOR Westry Green
STYLE DIRECTOR Elizabeth Mayhew
STYLIST Olga Naiman
PHOTO EDITOR Naomi Nista

PRESIDENT AND PUBLISHER Robin Domeniconi
VICE PRESIDENT, MARKETING AND BRAND STRATEGY
Grant Schneider
ASSOCIATE PUBLISHER, ADVERTISING Kevin White
GENERAL MANAGER Tina Pace
CONSUMER MARKETING DIRECTOR Kristiana Helmick
VICE PRESIDENT, PR AND COMMUNICATIONS
Kristen Jones Connell
PRODUCTION DIRECTOR Tracy Kelliher

TIME INC. HOME ENTERTAINMENT
PUBLISHER Richard Fraiman
EXECUTIVE DIRECTOR, MARKETING SERVICES Carol Pittard
DIRECTOR, RETAIL & SPECIAL SALES Tom Mifsud
MARKETING DIRECTOR, BRANDED BUSINESSES Swati Rao
DIRECTOR, NEW PRODUCT DEVELOPMENT Peter Harper
ASSISTANT FINANCIAL DIRECTOR Steven Sandonato
PREPRESS MANAGER Emily Rabin
PRODUCT MANAGER Victoria Alfonso
ASSOCIATE BOOK PRODUCTION MANAGER Suzanne Janso
ASSOCIATE PREPRESS MANAGER Anne-Michelle Gallero

SPECIAL THANKS Stephanie Abramson, Bozena Bannett,
Rachael Barrett, Alexandra Bliss, Glenn Buonocore, Daisy Cajas,
Bernadette Corbie, Pamela Grossman, Rachel Hardage, Michael
R. Hargreaves, Paul Hertel, Deanna Lowe, Noirin Lucas, Robert
Marasco, Tricia McGinty-Boyles, Brooke McGuire, Kate Merker,
Jacklyn Monk, Nancy Negovetich, Fon-Lin Nyeu, Melinda Page,
Jonathan Polsky, Alex Press, Ilene Schreider, Eva Spring, Sharon
Tanenbaum, Ashley Tate, Adriana Tierno, Sally Wadyka.

SPECIAL THANKS TO THE FOLLOWING STORES
ABC Carpet & Home, Aero, the Container Store, Côté France,
Country Swedish, Crate and Barrel, Holdeverything, Pottery
Barn, White on White.

COVER PHOTOGRAPHY David Prince
COVER STYLING Philippa Brathwaite
ILLUSTRATIONS Jason Lee

Published by Real Simple Books, a trademark of Time Inc.
1271 Avenue of the Americas, New York, NY 10020

First printing September 2005
ISBN: 1-932994-12-2
Library of Congress Catalog Control Number: 2005902454
Printed In China

We welcome your comments and suggestions about Real
Simple Books. Please e-mail us at books@realsimple.com, or
write to us at:

Real Simple Books
1271 Avenue of the Americas
Room 4139
New York, NY 10020

If you would like to order any of our hardcover edition books,
please call us at 800-327-6388 (Monday through Friday, 7:00
A.M. to 8:00 P.M. Central Time; or Saturday, 7:00 A.M. to 6:00 A.M.
Central Time).